Outstanding Achievement
in Drama
Junior Book Awards
May 21, 2013

Time Flies
and Other Short Plays

Also by David Ives

All in the Timing

Monsieur Eek

Time Flies
and Other Short Plays

By
DAVID IVES

Grove Press
New York

Published simultaneously in Canada
Printed in the United States of America

Library of Congress Cataloging-in-Publication Data
Ives, David
    Time flies and other short plays / by David Ives.
       p. cm.
    ISBN-10: 0-8021-3758-X
    ISBN-13: 978-0-8021-3758-6
    1. Title.
PS3559.V435 T5 2001
812'.54—dc21   00-042993

Grove Press
an imprint of Grove/Atlantic, Inc.
841 Broadway
New York, NY 10003
Distributed by Publishers Group West

08 09 10   10 9 8 7 6 5

CONTENTS

PREFACE

This volume brings together all the short plays I've written since an earlier anthology called *All In The Timing: Fourteen Plays*. Some of the plays in this new volume ("Time Flies," "Degas, C'est Moi," "Dr. Fritz," and the revised "Speed-the-Play") were part of an Off-Broadway evening called "Mere Mortals." Others ("Enigma Variations," "Twicknam," "Babel," "Soap Opera" and "Saints") made up another evening called "Lives Of The Saints." I'd be a damned ingrate if I didn't say that the creation of those two shows depended hugely upon the spectacular talents, patience and intelligence of director John Rando and a band of incomparable actors: Nancy Opel, Anne O'Sullivan, Arnie Burton, Danton Stone, Willis Sparks and Jessalyn Gilsig. They are as audible in those plays as I am. I also take this opportunity to tip my fedora to the Guggenheim Foundation for handing me a generous grant that saw me through the writing of the "Lives Of The Saints" evening.

Some origins, for anyone interested in such things. "Dr. Fritz" was sparked by a story in *The New York Times* about a South American mechanic-turned-healer who performs gruesome medical operations without anesthesia and using the crudest of tools while under the spiritual influence of a German doctor who died in 1912. Apparently, this works, so it may be the answer to America's health crisis. The idea for "Degas" simply came to me out of the blue as I woke up one Sunday morning. The moment I opened my eyes, the sentence *I decided to be Degas for a day* sounded in the porches of my ears. (All those delicious D's!) I went straight to my writing table and wrote the idea up as a 1,000-word humor piece. The day the piece appeared in the *Times* Magazine, John Guare called me up and said: "How could you waste this idea on *The New York Times?*" So I turned it into a play.

"Soap Opera" popped into my head as I stood on a totally empty street in Independence, Kansas—again on an early Sunday morning, interestingly enough—looking into an old shop window that had a poster of the weeping Maytag Repairman on display. Suddenly that well-known TV-commercial face seemed pathetic, even tragic— human. I did the instinctive human thing and tried to help turn his pain comedywards. My old David Mamet, um, *hommage* "Speed-the-Play" got updated, rethought, rehauled and rewritten thoroughly for the evening called "Mere Mortals." That revised version is included here for all disciples of The Fuckin' Master.

By now I've amassed pages and pages of ideas for plays—many too many plays for me to live long enough to write. But then, Cato The Elder had some excellent agricultural advice circa 200 B.C.: *Sterquilinium magnum stude ut habeas*, or: "Make sure you've got a nice big dungheap." Advice as valuable to writers as to farmers. (*Sterquilinium*'s a handsome word to throw around your next literary tea.) On an opposite advisory tack is another line I often ponder, which a priest in my high school used to quote with pointed relish. It's part of a letter Cicero sent to a servant who was getting the Roman politico's country house ready for the summer and works as well for playwrights chewing their pens as for sophomores chewing their futures: *Si aqua in balnia non sit, fac sit.* "If there's no water in the bath, put it there."

In a world where millions of people a night watch "Kojak" reruns in distant, silent communion every evening, one wonders about the future of a local, handmade art like theatre which can only touch, tickle or appall a roomful of people at a time. Independent movies have invaded and coopted the exotic psychic and existential terrain that once belonged solely to good theatre. Smart young writers by-pass the boards and head straight for Gomorrah, to set up shop in an office in West Hollywood. In New York it's practically impossible to cast a play these days, when movie, TV and commercial commitments mean that only three unsuitable actors over the age of twenty-three are available and willing to commit to four weeks of rehearsal and a limited run at insulting wages. "The theatre," a notable Hollywood producer is reputed to have said, "is nothing but a flea up an elephant's ass." And yet somehow fine plays still get written and good theatre continues to get made and actors still come back to speak lines in front of that handful of diehards. Must be one hell of a flea.

In the several years since my last anthology of short plays, Eugene Ionesco died, still a wildly undervalued poet of the theatre. One obituary quoted his own reasons for still sitting down to work in this wacky masochistic business: "To allow others to share in the astonishment of being, the dazzlement of existence, and to shout to God and other human beings our anguish, letting it be known that we were there."

Now pardon me while I go tend my dungheap and fill up the bath.

TIME FLIES

this play is for
John Rando,
Anne O'Sullivan, Arnie Burton
and Willis Sparks,
who made it fly

Evening. A pond. The chirr of tree toads, and the buzz of a huge swarm of insects. Upstage, a thicket of tall cattails. Downstage, a deep green love seat. Overhead, an enormous full moon.

A loud cuckoo sounds, like the mechanical "cuckoo" of a clock.

Lights come up on two mayflies: HORACE *and* MAY, *buzzing as they "fly" in. They are dressed like singles on an evening out, he in a jacket and tie, she in a party dress—but they have insectlike antennae; long tubelike tails; and on their backs, translucent wings. Outsized horn-rim glasses give the impression of very large eyes. May has distinctly hairy legs.*

HORACE & MAY   Bzzzzzzzzzzzzzzzzzz . . .

Their wings stop fluttering, as they "settle."

MAY   Well here we are. This is my place.

HORACE   Already? That was fast.

MAY   Swell party, huh.

HORACE   Yeah. Quite a swarm.

MAY   Thank you for flying me home.

HORACE   No. Sure. I'm happy to. Absolutely. My pleasure. I mean—you're very, very, very welcome.

Their eyes lock and they near each other as if for a kiss, their wings fluttering a little.

Bzzzzzzzz . . .

MAY   Bzzzzzzzz . . .

Before their jaws can meet: "CUCKOO!"—and Horace breaks away.

HORACE   It's that late, is it. Anyway, it was very nice meeting you—I'm sorry, is it April?

MAY   May.

HORACE   May. Yes. Later than I thought, huh.

3

They laugh politely.

MAY   That's very funny, Vergil.

HORACE   It's Horace, actually.

MAY   I'm sorry. The buzz at that party was so loud.

HORACE   So you're "May the mayfly."

MAY   Yeah. Guess my parents didn't have much imagination. May, mayfly.

HORACE   You don't, ah, live with your parents, do you, May?

MAY   No, my parents died around dawn this morning.

HORACE   Isn't that funny. Mine died around dawn too.

MAY   Maybe it's fate.

HORACE   Is that what it izzzzzzzz . . . ?

MAY   Bzzzzzzzz. . . .

HORACE   Bzzzzzzzzzzzzzz . . .

They near for a kiss, but Horace breaks away.

   Well, I'd better be going now. Good night.

MAY   Do you want a drink?

HORACE   I'd love a drink, actually . . .

MAY   Let me just turn on a couple of fireflies. (*May tickles the underside of a couple of TWO-FOOT-LONG FIREFLIES hanging like a chandelier, and the fireflies light up.*)

HORACE   Wow. Great pond! (*indicating the love seat*) I love the lily pad.

MAY   The lily pad was here. It kinda grew on me. (*polite laugh*) Care to take the load off your wings?

4

HORACE That's all right. I'll just—you know—hover. But will you look at that . . . ! (*Turning, Horace bats May with his wings.*)

MAY Oof!

HORACE I'm sorry. Did we collide?

MAY No. No. It's fine.

HORACE I've only had my wings about six hours.

MAY Really! So have I . . . ! Wasn't molting disgusting?

HORACE Eugh. I'm glad that's over.

MAY Care for some music? I've got The Beatles, The Byrds, The Crickets . . .

HORACE I love the Crickets.

MAY Well so do I . . . (*She kicks a large, insect-shaped coffee table, and we hear the buzz of crickets.*)

HORACE (*as they boogie to that*) So are you going out with any—I mean, are there any other mayflies in the neighborhood?

MAY No, it's mostly wasps.

HORACE So, you live here by your, um, all by yourself? Alone?

MAY All by my lonesome.

HORACE And will you look at that moon.

MAY You know that's the first moon I've ever seen?

HORACE That's the first moon *I've* ever seen . . . !

MAY Isn't that funny.

HORACE When were you born?

MAY About seven-thirty this morning.

HORACE So was I! Seven thirty-three!

MAY Isn't that funny.

HORACE Or maybe it's fate.

They near each other again, as if for a kiss.

　Bzzzzzzz . . .

MAY Bzzzzzzzzz . . . I think that moon is having a very emotional effect on me.

HORACE Me too.

MAY It must be nature.

HORACE Me too.

MAY Or maybe it's fate.

HORACE Me too . . .

MAY Bzzzzzzzzzz . . .

HORACE Bzzzzzzzzzzzzzz . . .

They draw their tails very close. Suddenly:

A FROG *(amplified, over loudspeaker)* Ribbit, ribbit!

HORACE A frog!

MAY A frog!

HORACE & MAY The frogs are coming, the frogs are coming! *(They "fly" around the stage in a panic. Ad lib:)* A frog, a frog! The frogs are coming, the frogs are coming! *(They finally stop, breathless.)*

MAY It's okay. It's okay.

HORACE Oh my goodness.

MAY I think he's gone now.

HORACE Oh my goodness, that scared me.

MAY That is the only drawback to living here. The frogs.

HORACE You know, I like frog films and frog literature. I just don't like frogs.

MAY And they're so rude if you're not a frog yourself.

HORACE Look at me. I'm shaking.

MAY Why don't I fix you something. Would you like a grasshopper? Or a stinger?

HORACE Just some stagnant water would be fine.

MAY A little duckweed in that? Some algae?

HORACE Straight up is fine.

MAY (*as she pours his drink*) Sure I couldn't tempt you to try the lily pad?

HORACE Well, maybe for just a second. (*Horace flutters down onto the love seat:*) Zzzzzzz . . .

MAY (*handing him a glass*) Here you go. Cheers, Horace.

HORACE Long life, May.

They clink glasses.

MAY Do you want to watch some tube?

HORACE Sure. What's on?

MAY Let's see. (*She checks a green TV Guide.*) There is . . . "The Love Bug." "M. Butterfly." "The Spider's Stratagem." "Travels With My Ant." "Angels and Insects." "The Fly . . ."

HORACE The original, or Jeff Goldblum?

MAY Jeff Goldblum.

HORACE Eugh. Too gruesome.

MAY "Born Yesterday." And "Life on Earth."

HORACE What's on that?

MAY   "Swamp Life," with Sir David Attenborough.

HORACE   That sounds good.

MAY   Shall we try it?

HORACE   Carpe diem.

MAY   Carpe diem? What's that?

HORACE   I don't know. It's Latin.

MAY   What's Latin?

HORACE   I don't know. I'm just a mayfly.

"Cuckoo!"

And we're right on time for it.

May presses a remote control and DAVID ATTENBOROUGH *appears, wearing a safari jacket.*

DAVID ATTENBOROUGH   Hello, I'm David Attenborough. Welcome to "Swamp Life."

MAY   Isn't this comfy.

HORACE   Is my wing in your way?

MAY   No. It's fine.

DAVID ATTENBOROUGH   You may not believe it, but within this seemingly lifeless puddle, there thrives a teeming world of vibrant life.

HORACE   May, look—isn't that your pond?

MAY   I think that is my pond!

HORACE   He said "puddle."

DAVID ATTENBOROUGH   This puddle is only several inches across, but its stagnant water plays host to over fourteen gazillion different species.

MAY   It is my pond!

DAVID ATTENBOROUGH   Every species here is engaged in a constant, desperate battle for survival. Feeding—meeting—mating—breeding—dying. And mating. And meeting. And mating. And feeding. And dying. Mating. Mating. Meeting. Breeding. Brooding. Braiding—those that can braid. Feeding. Mating . . .

MAY   All right, Sir Dave!

DAVID ATTENBOROUGH   Mating, mating, mating, and mating.

HORACE   Only one thing on his mind.

MAY   The filth on television these days.

DAVID ATTENBOROUGH   Tonight we start off with one of the saddest creatures of this environment.

HORACE   The dung beetle.

MAY   The toad.

DAVID ATTENBOROUGH   The lowly mayfly.

HORACE   Did he say "the mayfly"?

MAY   I think he said "the *lowly* mayfly."

DAVID ATTENBOROUGH   Yes. The lowly mayfly. Like these two mayflies, for instance.

HORACE   May—I think that's us!

MAY   Oh my God . . .

HORACE & MAY (*together*)   We're on television!

HORACE   I don't believe it!

MAY   I wish my mother was here to see this!

HORACE   This is amazing!

MAY   Oh God, I look terrible!

HORACE   You look very good.

MAY   I can't look at this.

DAVID ATTENBOROUGH   As you can see, the lowly mayfly is not one of nature's most attractive creatures.

MAY   At least we don't wear safari jackets.

HORACE   I wish he'd stop saying "lowly mayfly."

DAVID ATTENBOROUGH   The lowly mayfly has a very distinctive khkhkhkhkhkhkhkhkhkkh . . . (*He makes the sound of TV "static."*)

MAY   I think there's something wrong with my antenna . . . (*She adjusts the antenna on her head.*)

HORACE   You don't have cable?

MAY   Not on this pond.

DAVID ATTENBOROUGH   (*stops the static sound*)   . . . and sixty tons of droppings.

HORACE   That fixed it.

MAY   Can I offer you some food? I've got some plankton in the pond. And some very nice gnat.

HORACE   I do love good gnat.

MAY   I'll set it out, you can pick. (*She rises and gets some food, as:*)

DAVID ATTENBOROUGH   The lowly mayfly first appeared some 350 million years ago . . .

MAY   That's impressive.

DAVID ATTENBOROUGH   . . . and is of the order Ephemeroptera, meaning, "living for a single day."

MAY   I did not know that!

HORACE   "Living for a single day." Huh . . .

MAY (*setting out a tray on the coffee table*)   There you go.

HORACE   Gosh, May. That's beautiful.

MAY   There's curried gnat, salted gnat, Scottish smoked gnat . . .

HORACE   I love that.

MAY   . . . gnat with pesto, gnat au naturelle, and Gnat King Cole.

HORACE   I don't think I could finish a whole one.

MAY   "Gnat" to worry.

They laugh politely.

That's larva dip there in the center. Just dig in.

DAVID ATTENBOROUGH   As for the life of the common mayfly . . .

HORACE   Oh. We're "common" now.

DAVID ATTENBOROUGH   . . . it is a simple round of meeting, mating, meeting, mating—

MAY   Here we go again.

DAVID ATTENBOROUGH   —breeding, feeding, feeding . . .

HORACE   This dip is fabulous.

DAVID ATTENBOROUGH   . . . and dying.

MAY   Leaf?

HORACE   Thank you.

May breaks a leaf off a plant and hands it to Horace.

DAVID ATTENBOROUGH   Mayflies are a major food source for trout and salmon.

MAY   Will you look at that savagery?

HORACE   That poor, poor mayfly.

DAVID ATTENBOROUGH Fishermen like to bait hooks with mayfly look-alikes.

MAY Bastards!—Excuse me.

DAVID ATTENBOROUGH And then there is the giant bullfrog.

FROG (*amplified, over loudspeaker*) Ribbit, ribbit!

HORACE & MAY The frogs are coming, the frogs are coming!

They "fly" around the stage in a panic—and end up "flying" right into each other's arms.

HORACE Well there.

MAY Hello.

DAVID ATTENBOROUGH Welcome to "Swamp Life." (*David Attenborough exits.*)

MAY (*hypnotized by Horace*) Funny how we flew right into each other's wings.

HORACE It is funny.

MAY Or fate.

HORACE Do you think he's gone?

MAY David Attenborough?

HORACE The frog.

MAY What frog. Bzzzz . . .

HORACE Bzzzzz . . .

DAVID ATTENBOROUGH'S VOICE As you see, mayflies can be quite affectionate . . .

HORACE & MAY Bzzzzzzzzzzzz . . .

DAVID ATTENBOROUGH'S VOICE . . . mutually palpating their proboscises.

HORACE You know, I've been wanting to palpate your proboscis all evening.

MAY I think it was larva at first sight.

HORACE & MAY (*rubbing proboscises together*)
Zzzzzzzzzzzzzzzzzzzzzzzzzzzz . . .

MAY (*very British, "Brief Encounter"*) Oh darling, darling.

HORACE Oh do darling do let's always be good to each other, shall we?

MAY Let's do do that, darling, always, always.

HORACE Always?

MAY Always.

HORACE & MAY Zzzzzzzzzzzzzzzzzzzzzzzzzzzzzzzzzzzz!

MAY Rub my antennae. Rub my antennae. (*Horace rubs May's antennae with his hands.*)

DAVID ATTENBOROUGH'S VOICE Sometimes mayflies rub antennae together.

MAY Oh yes. Yes. Just like that. Yes. Keep going. Harder. Rub harder.

HORACE Rub mine now. Rub my antennae. Oh yes. Yes. Yes. Yes. There's the rub. There's the rub. Go. Go. Go!

DAVID ATTENBOROUGH'S VOICE Isn't that a picture. Now get a load of mating.

Horace gets into mounting position, behind May. He rubs her antennae while she wolfs down the gnat-food in front of her.

HORACE & MAY Bzzzzzzzzzzzzzzzzzzzzzzzzzzzzzzzzzzzzzzz!

DAVID ATTENBOROUGH'S VOICE Unfortunately for this insect, the mayfly has a life span of only one day.

Horace and May stop buzzing, abruptly.

HORACE What was that . . . ?

DAVID ATTENBOROUGH'S VOICE The mayfly has a life span of only one day—living just long enough to meet, mate, have offspring, and die.

MAY Did he say "meet, mate, have offspring, and DIE"—?

DAVID ATTENBOROUGH'S VOICE I did. In fact, mayflies born at seven-thirty in the morning will die by the next dawn.

HORACE (*whimpers softly at the thought.*)

DAVID ATTENBOROUGH'S VOICE But so much for the lowly mayfly. Let's move on to the newt.

"Cuckoo!"

HORACE & MAY We're going to die . . . We're going to die! Mayday, mayday! We're going to die, we're going to die!

Weeping and wailing, they kneel, beat their breasts, cross themselves, daven, and tear their hair.

"Cuckoo!"

HORACE What time is it? What time is it?

MAY I don't wear a watch. I'm a lowly mayfly!

HORACE (*weeping*) Wah-ha-ha-ha!

MAY (*suddenly sober*) Well isn't this beautiful.

HORACE (*gasping for breath*) Oh my goodness. I think I'm having an asthma attack. Can mayflies have asthma?

MAY I don't know. Ask Mr. Safari Jacket.

HORACE Maybe if I put a paper bag over my head . . .

MAY So this is my sex life?

HORACE Do you have a paper bag?

MAY One bang, a bambino, and boom—that's it?

HORACE Do you have a paper bag?

MAY For the common mayfly, foreplay segues right into funeral.

HORACE Do you have a paper bag?

MAY I don't have time to look for a paper bag, I'm going to be *dead* very shortly, all right?

"Cuckoo!"

HORACE Oh come on! That wasn't a whole hour!

"Cuckoo!"

Time is moving so fast now.

"Cuckoo!"

HORACE & MAY Shut up!

"Cuckoo!"

HORACE (*suddenly sober*) This explains everything. We were born this morning, we hit puberty in mid-afternoon, our biological clocks went BONG, and here we are. Hot to copulate.

MAY For the one brief miserable time we get to do it.

HORACE Yeah.

MAY Talk about a quickie.

HORACE Wait a minute, wait a minute.

MAY Talk fast.

HORACE What makes you think it would be so brief?

MAY Oh, I'm sorry. Did I insult your vast sexual experience?

HORACE Are you more experienced than I am, Dr. Ruth? Luring me here to your pad?

MAY I see. I see. Blame me!

HORACE Can I remind you we only get one shot at this?

MAY So I can rule out multiple orgasms, is that it?

HORACE I'm just saying there's not a lot of time to hone one's erotic technique, okay?

MAY Hmp!

HORACE And I'm trying to sort out some very big entomontological questions here rather quickly, do you mind?

MAY And I'm just the babe here, is that it? I'm just a piece of tail.

HORACE I'm not the one who suggested TV.

MAY I'm not the one who wanted to watch "Life On Earth." "Oh—'Swamp Life.' That sounds *interesting.*"

FROG Ribbit, ribbit.

HORACE *(calmly)* There's a frog up there.

MAY Oh, I'm really scared. I'm terrified.

FROG Ribbit, ribbit!

HORACE *(calling to the frog)* We're right down here! Come and get us!

MAY Breeding. Dying. Breeding. Dying. So this is the whole purpose of mayflies? To make more mayflies?

HORACE Does the world *need* more mayflies?

MAY We're a major food source for trout and salmon.

HORACE How nice for the salmon.

MAY Do you want more food?

HORACE I've lost a bit of my appetite, all right?

MAY Oh. Excuse me.

HORACE I'm sorry. Really, May.

MAY (*starts to cry*) Males!

HORACE Leaf?

He plucks another leaf and hands it to her.

MAY Thank you.

HORACE Really. I didn't mean to snap at you.

MAY Oh, you've been very nice.

"CUCKOO!" They jump.

Under the circumstances.

HORACE I'm sorry.

MAY No, I'm sorry.

HORACE No, I'm sorry.

MAY No, I'm sorry.

HORACE No, I'm sorry.

MAY We'd better stop apologizing, we're going to be dead soon.

HORACE I'm sorry.

MAY Oh Horace, I had such plans. I had such wonderful plans. I wanted to see Paris.

HORACE What's Paris?

MAY I have no fucking idea.

HORACE Maybe we'll come back as caviar and find out.

They laugh a little at that.

I was just hoping to live till Tuesday.

MAY (*making a small joke*) What's a Tuesday?

They laugh a little more at that.

The sun's going to be up soon. I'm scared, Horace. I'm so scared.

HORACE   You know, May, we don't have much time, and really, we hardly know each other—but I'm going to say it. I think you're swell. I think you're divine. From your buggy eyes to the thick raspy hair on your legs to the intoxicating scent of your secretions.

MAY   Eeeuw.

HORACE   Eeeuw? No. I say *woof*. And I say who cares if life is a swamp and we're just a couple of small bugs in a very small pond. I say live, May! I say . . . darn it . . . live!

MAY   But how?

HORACE   Well, I don't honestly know that . . .

Attenborough appears.

DAVID ATTENBOROUGH   You could fly to Paris.

MAY   We could fly to Paris!

HORACE   Do we have time to fly to Paris?

MAY   Carpe diem!

HORACE   What is carpe diem?

DAVID ATTENBOROUGH   It means "bon voyage."

HORACE & MAY   And we're outta here!

They fly off to Paris as . . .

BLACKOUT.

DEGAS, C'EST MOI

this play is for Martha, of course

ED, *on a bed, asleep. An alarm clock goes off. He doesn't move. Then, he is suddenly awake.*

ED   A stroke of genius. I decide to be Degas for a day. Edgar Degas. Why Degas? says a pesky little voice at the back of my head. Well why *not* Degas? Pourquoi pas Degas? Maybe the prismatic bars of color on my ceiling have inspired me.

We see prismatic bars of color.

Maybe the creamy white light spreading on my walls has moved me.

Creamy white light spreads on the wall.

Maybe it's all this cheap French wine I been drinking. (*He finds a wine bottle in his bed.*) Anyway I don't have to explain myself. Yes! Today, I will be Edgar Degas!—Is it Ed*gar,* or Ed*ouard*? Okay, so I don't know much about Degas. Let's see. Dead, French, impressionist painter of, what, jockeys, ballerinas, flowers, that kinda thing. And okay granted, I'm not French, dead, or a painter of any kind. Not a lotta common ground. And yet, and yet—are Degas and I not united by our shared humanity? By our common need for love, coffee, and deodorant?

DORIS *enters.*

DORIS   Oh God, oh God, oh God. Have you seen my glasses?

ED   Doris breaks in on my inspiration.

DORIS   I can't find my glasses.

ED   Doris, I say to Doris, I'm going to be Degas today.

DORIS   He's gonna kill me if I'm late again.

ED   Doris doesn't see the brilliance of the idea.

DORIS   This is a tragedy.

ED   Doris—I am Degas!

DORIS You're what?

ED Is it Edgar or Edward? It's Edgar, isn't it.

DORIS Don't forget the dry cleaning. (*Doris kisses him.*) 'Bye. (*Doris exits.*)

ED Alas, poor Doris. Distracted by the banal. No matter. I start my day and brush my teeth as Degas. (*Ed hops out of bed and produces a green toothbrush. The bed disappears.*) Oh man. This is wonderful! In the bathroom, everything seems transformed yet nothing has changed. The very porcelain pullulates with possibilities. Will you look at the lustre of that toilet? And the light on that green plastic! The bristles are disgusting, but the light is fantastic! (*French accent:*) Per'aps I weel paint you later.

We hear the sound of a shower.

In the shower, it feels strange, lathering an immortal. What's even stranger, the immortal is lathering back. How did I become such a genius? I, who flunked woodshop in high school? Was it my traumatic childhood? Did I *have* a traumatic childhood? There was Uncle Stosh's unfortunate party trick with the parakeet. *Ouch.* Well something must've happened. Because now I'm great. I'm brilliant. My name will live forever! (*He considers that a second.*) Whoo. Wow. This is too big for even me to contemplate. I go out into the world with dry cleaning.

He grabs some clothing as we hear city noises, car horns, etcetera.

O glorious polychromatic city! Gone the dreary daily déjà vu. Today—*Degas* vu!

A DRIVER enters at a run, holding a steering wheel, headed right for Ed. Loud car horn and screeching brakes heard as Ed dodges aside.

DRIVER Moron!

ED Idiot!

DRIVER   Jerk! Watch where you're going!

ED   Do you know who you almost killed?

DRIVER   Yeah! An *asshole!* (*Driver exits.*)

ED   Another couple of inches and the world would've lost a hundred masterpieces.

DRY CLEANER *enters, writing on a pad.*

DRY CLEANER   Okay, what's the dirt today?

ED   At the dry cleaner's I notice something strange . . .

DRY CLEANER (*taking the dry cleaning*)   One shirt, one skirt, one jacket.

ED   My dry cleaner acts exactly the same.

DRY CLEANER   You know you need some serious reweaving?

ED   Madam, how I would love to capture you in charcoal.

DRY CLEANER   My husband already caught me in puce. (*Tears a sheet off the pad.*) After five.

The Dry Cleaner exits with the clothing.

ED   She gives not a flutter of recognition. Then on the corner, the newsguy tries to sell me my paper just like always.

NEWSGUY *enters.*

NEWSGUY   *Daily Noose?*

ED   Actually, have you got anything *en française?*

NEWSGUY   Let's see, I got *Le Mot, Le Monde, Le Reve, Le Chat, La Chasse, L'Abime,* and *Mademoiselle Boom Boom.*

ED   I'll just take the *News.*

NEWSGUY   Change. (*He flips an invisible coin, which Ed "catches," then the Newsguy exits.*)

ED   Still not a blink of recognition. Then as I head down Broadway, people pass me by without a second glance. Or even a first glance.

PEOPLE *enter and pass him.*

I might as well be invisible. I, Edgar Degas! And then I realize with a shock: *It makes no difference to be Degas.* To all these people, I could be anyone! And if I'm anyone—who are all these people?

MORE PEOPLE *pass him.*

And yet . . . And yet maybe the other Degas walked this invisibly through Paris.

We hear a French accordion and the clip-clop of horses.

Maybe he too was rudely bumped into by the bourgeoisie on the upper Left Bank . . .

A PEDESTRIAN *bumps into him as a* WORKER *enters carrying a crate loaded with cabbages.*

Shouted at by workers at the Food City de Montparnasse . . .

WORKER   Watcha back, watcha back! (*Worker exits.*)

ED   Cursed by the less fortunate.

HOMELESS PERSON *enters.*

HOMELESS PERSON   *Fuck* you. *Fuck* you.

ED   And you know, there's a kind of comfort in this.

HOMELESS PERSON   *Fuck* you.

ED   Completely anonymous, I'm free to appreciate the gray cloud of pigeons overhead . . .

We hear the cooing of pigeons.

The impasto at Ray's Pizza . . .

PIZZA MAN *Pepperoni!*

ED The chiaroscuro of the M-Eleven bus . . .

LOUD MOTOR of a city bus.

Nobody knows it, but I am walking down this street with a jewel cupped in my hands. The secret precious jewel of my talent.

UNEMPLOYMENT WORKER *enters.*

UNEMPLOYMENT WORKER Next!

ED My delicious anonymity continues at Unemployment.

Accordion and horses stop as a sign descends which says, "UNEMPLOYMENT LINE HERE."

UNEMPLOYMENT WORKER Sign your claim at the bottom, please.

ED Do you notice the name I signed in the bottom right corner?

UNEMPLOYMENT WORKER Edgar Day-hass. Edgar Deejis. Edgar Deggis. Edgar De Gas. Edgar De What?

ED Edgar Degas. And—?

UNEMPLOYMENT WORKER *And*—this name at the bottom does not match the name at the top of the form.

ED No, no, no, no . . .

UNEMPLOYMENT WORKER Are you not the same person as the person at the top of the form?

ED I am a person at the top of *my* form. I am *Edgar. Degas.*

UNEMPLOYMENT WORKER The dead French painter?

ED The same.

UNEMPLOYMENT WORKER Next!

Unemployment Worker exits and the sign goes away.

ED Recalling my painterly interest in racetracks, I stop off at OTB.

OTB WORKER enters.

OTB WORKER Next!

ED Ten francs on Windmill, *s'il vous plaît.*

OTB WORKER *Oh mais oui, monsieur.*

ED Windmill—I say to him—because the jockey wears brilliant silks of crimson and gold. Windmill—I tell the man—because her sable flanks flash like lightning in the field. Windmill—I continue—because in form and moving she doth express an angel.

OTB WORKER *(handing over the betting slip)* Windmill—

ED —he says to me—

OTB WORKER —always comes in last.

RACING BELL.

ED And Windmill does.

BUZZER.

But who gives a shit? *(Tears up the betting slip.)* I'm Degas!

OTB Worker exits. Ed looks around.

Oh—the library. Maybe I should look myself up.

A sign descends: "SILENCE." A LIBRARIAN enters.

LIBRARIAN *Shhhhhh!*

ED Excuse me. Have you got anything on Degas?

LIBRARIAN Degas. You mean the crassly conservative counterfeminist patriarchal pedophile painter?

ED No, I mean the colorist who chronicled his age and who continues to inspire through countless posters, postcards and T-shirts.

LIBRARIAN Section D, aisle two.

ED Patriarchal pedoph—

LIBRARIAN *QUIET! (Librarian exits.)*

ED But who needs the carping of critics, the lies of biographers? I know who I am. Famished by creativity, I stop at Twin Donut.

Two tables appear. A YOUNG WOMAN sits at one, writing in a journal. Ed sits at the other.

TWIN DONUT WORKER *(enters with a plate)* Vanilla cruller!

ED So there I am, scribbling a priceless doodle on my napkin, when I notice someone staring at me.

The Young Woman stops writing and looks at Ed.

A young woman writing in a journal. Has she recognized me? She smiles slightly. Yes. She knows I am Degas. Not only that. *(He looks again. The Young Woman starts writing.)* She *loves* Degas. That one look has redeemed all my years of effort. My work has given meaning to someone's life. Should I seduce her? It would be traditional.

A schmaltzy-romantic violin is heard.

YOUNG WOMAN *(writing)* "April six. Twin Donut. Just saw Edgar Degas two tables over. So he likes vanilla crullers too! Suddenly this day is glorious and memorable. Would love to lie in bed all afternoon and make l'amour with Degas . . ."

ED But no. I'd only cast her off, break her heart. Not to mention what it would do to Doris.

YOUNG WOMAN *(writing)* "Dwayne would kill me."

ED But isn't it my duty as an artist to seduce this girl? Experience life to the fullest . . . ?

YOUNG WOMAN Adieu.

ED   Adieu.

Young Woman exits

Too late.

Tables disappear. Afternoon light.

On Fifth Avenue, a mysterious figure passes, leading a
Doberman. Or vice versa.

*A FIGURE in a raincoat, hat and sunglasses, holding a stiffened leash, as
if a dog were on it, crosses.*

It's somebody famous. But who? Kissinger? Woody Allen?
Oprah?

Figure exits.

Whoa, whoa, whoa, just for a picosecond there, I forget
who I am! Just for a moment—I seem to be nobody. The labor
of hanging onto one's identity!

Empty picture frames descend and a MUSEUM GUARD enters.

At the museum I am simply amazed to find how much I
accomplished—even without television.

A Degas self-portrait appears.

What's this . . . Ah. A self-portrait. Not a great likeness, maybe.
But so full of . . . what? . . . *feeling*. I stare into my fathomless eyes.

A MUSEUMGOER stands beside him looking at the portrait.

MUSEUMGOER   Mmm.

ED   Mmmmmmm.

MUSEUMGOER   Bit smudgy, isn't it?

ED   "Smudgy"?

MUSEUMGOER This area in here.

ED Yeah, but what about this area over here?

MUSEUMGOER No, but look at this area here. This is smudge.

ED Okay. So I had an off day.

MUSEUMGOER An "off day" . . . ?

ED Not all my work was perfect.

MUSEUMGOER Indeed. How could it be . . . ? (*The Museumgoer slips away.*)

ED Philistine. Probably headed for van Gogh. To kneel in adoration at the sunflowers. I couldn't believe it, the day he started signing his paintings "Vincent." "*Vince*," we called him. What a jerk.

Degas's WOMAN WITH CRYSANTHEMUMS *appears.*

Ah yes. *Woman with Chrysanthemums.* A personal favorite among my masterworks. God, when I remember that morning over a century ago . . . Can it be that long now? This was an empty canvas and I stood in front it paralyzed by its whiteness. Then I reached for my brush . . .

He produces a paintbrush.

. . . and the picture crystallized. In a moment I saw it all. This pensive woman, oblivious of the transcendent burst of color right at her shoulder. The natural exuberance of the flowers alongside her human sorrow. Yes. Yes! Our blindness to the beautiful! Our insensibility to the splendor right there within our reach!

MUSEUM GUARD Step back, please.

ED Excuse me?

MUSEUM GUARD You have to step back, sir. You're too close to the painting.

ED I'm too close to this painting . . . ?

MUSEUM GUARD Do you copy?

ED No, I don't copy. I am an original!

MUSEUM GUARD Sir?

ED I step back.

He does so, and the Guard exits.

But the glow of my exaltation stays with me all the way to the Akropolis Diner . . .

A table appears. Doris enters.

DORIS Oh God, oh God.

ED . . . where Doris meets me for dinner.

DORIS What a day.

ED What a fabulous day. Epic!

DORIS Six hours of xeroxing.

ED No, listen. Degas. Remember?

DORIS Degas . . . ?

ED I've been Degas all day.

DORIS The toilets erupted again. The women's room was like Vesuvius.

ED I *am* Degas.

DORIS They were going to fix those toilets last week.

ED As Doris dilates on toilets, I begin to feel Degas slip away a little . . .

DORIS Waiter!

ED . . . like a second skin I'm shedding . . .

DORIS Waiter!

ED . . . leaving nothing behind.

DORIS Where is that guy?

ED Then I see a man at another table, staring at me. Looking at me with such pity. Such unalloyed human sympathy.

DORIS At least I found my glasses.

ED And then I realize.

DORIS They were in my purse all the time.

ED The man is Renoir.

DORIS (*holding up her glasses*) See?

ED By now, Degas is completely gone.

Light changes to night light as Ed and Doris rise.

Doris and I walk home in silence.

Doris exits. Lights darken to a single spot on Ed.

People say they have a voice inside their heads. The voice that tells themselves the story of their lives. Now I'm walking up the street, now I'm taking out my key, when did that streetlight burn out, is there a meaning to all this, who's that person coming down the stairs, now I'm putting my key in the door, now I do this, now I do that. The facts of our lives. Yes, I too have always had a voice like that in my head. But now, tonight, no one is listening. That presence that always listened in at the back of my mind is no longer there. Nor is there a presence behind that presence listening in. Nor a presence behind that, nor behind that, nor behind that. All the way back to the back of my mind, no one is listening in. The story of my life is going on unwatched. Unheard. I am alone.

The bed appears. Ed sprawls on it.

I find myself upstairs, sprawled on the bed while Doris runs the bathwater. Degas is dust. All my glory, all my fame, all my achievements are utterly forgotten. Immortality? A cruel joke. The jewel I bore through the streets in the cup of my hands is gone, and my hands are empty. I have done nothing. Absolutely nothing.

A light comes up on Doris, drying herself with a towel.

Then I find myself looking through the doorway into the bathroom and I see Doris standing naked with her foot up on the edge of the old lion-footed tub, drying herself. The overhead light is dim, but Doris is fluorescent—radiant—luminous—with pinks and lavenders and vermilions playing over her skin. The frayed towel she's wrapped in gleams like a rose. She turns and looks back at me and smiles.

Doris turns and looks over her shoulder at Ed.

DORIS Bonsoir, Degas.

ED Degas? Who needs him?

He holds his hand out to her across the intervening space, and she holds hers out to him. The lights fade.

DR. FRITZ, OR:
THE FORCES OF LIGHT

this play was written for
and is dedicated to
the incomparable Nancy Opel

MARIA *is sitting behind a crude plank table made from an old door. She wears a plain white linen smock and huaraches. She is knitting— but without any yarn. The needles click. On a rack beside her is a raggedy homemade doll with outstretched arms. Over the room hangs a rusty meathook. Upstage: a picture of Jesus as the Sacred Heart.*

MARIA *(sings, softly, calmly)* Corazona!
Corazona di Cristu!
Wer bist Du?
Wer bist Du . . . ?

TOM *enters, bent over at the waist, holding his side and gasping in pain. He is dressed in Bermuda shorts, expensive sandals, and a T-shirt that says, "WELLCOM TO BONA FORTUNA!"*

TOM *Eugh. Eugh. Eugh.*

MARIA Bendio, sinhors! Comari *ta*?

TOM *Eugh.*

MARIA How you are feeling todays?

TOM *Eugh.*

MARIA You want to buy a souvenirs?

TOM *Eugh.*

MARIA One of a kinds.

TOM I'm looking for Dr. Fritz.

MARIA Ah, Dr. Fritz can cure everything. You have a troothache?

TOM No. Poison.

MARIA You have been poisoned? Tsk, tsk, tsk, tsk.

TOM Food poisoning.

MARIA Oh, the food poisonings. But no troothache?

TOM *I don't have a goddamn toothache.*

MARIA Eh, eh, eh. This is not nice languages, Pablo.

TOM Pablo?

MARIA I was foretold of a man named Pablo coming with a troothache.

TOM I'm not Pablo.

MARIA This is why you have no troothache.

TOM Look . . .

MARIA *(looking behind herself)* Where?

TOM Listen . . .

MARIA *(puts a hand to her ear)* I hear nothings.

TOM My name is Tom Sanders. At the hotel I talked to this man Pedro . . .

MARIA Pedro the doorman or Pedro the cook?

TOM Pedro the cook.

MARIA He so nice. You want to buy a souvenirs?

TOM No, thank you.

MARIA One of a kinds.

TOM Pedro said come here and ask for Dr. Fritz.

MARIA Ah, Dr. Fritz can cure everything. Broken bone, bullet hole, burn, amputation, housemaid's knee.

TOM But—

MARIA Terminal diseases is more difficult.

TOM But—

MARIA This is why they are called terminal.

TOM But—

MARIA Ah, but are they terminal? A case for Dr. Fritz.

TOM But—doesn't the sign say "BUTCHER"?

MARIA You speak the languages so good.

TOM *Eugh.*

MARIA Now this is the souvenir shop of Maria, and the offices of Dr. Fritz.

TOM (*pain*) Jesus Christ . . . !

MARIA (*turning to look*) Where?

TOM Is he here?

MARIA Jesus are everywhere.

TOM *Dr. Fritz.*

MARIA Oh, Dr. Fritz.

TOM Do you have a chair?

MARIA Only the chairs I am sitting on.

TOM Can I sit on it?

MARIA This is Dr. Fritz's chairs.

TOM Wait a minute. *You're* not Dr. Fritz . . . ?

MARIA I am the assistant of Dr. Fritz. (*laughs madly; then calm again*) At the moment.

TOM Oh God . . .

MARIA Good! You believe in God.

TOM What?

MARIA I say, Good! You believe in God.

TOM No I don't believe in God.

MARIA   But sinhors, you called on God, you said, Oh God, oh God.

TOM   It was a figure of speech, okay?

MARIA   You believe in Buddha? Buddha is good.

TOM   No.

MARIA   Krishna, maybe?

TOM   *No.*

MARIA   Just checking.

We hear a ringing, like a telephone.

TOM   What's that?

MARIA   What is what, sinhors?

RING.

TOM   Like a telephone.

MARIA   I hear nothings.

RING.

Maybe the food poisoning make you a little *lo*coco.

RING.

TOM   Don't you hear that bell?

MARIA   Oh, the bells. (*picks up a souvenir doll and speaks into it like a telephone*) Mushi mushi . . . Si . . . Si . . . Si . . . Dosvee*don*yeh. (*hangs up the doll*) This was Pedro. He say you are on the way.

TOM *picks up the doll and looks at it.*

There is always more meat than meets the eyes meat, no?

TOM   I must have fever.

MARIA   Are you shvitzing?

TOM I am shvitzing.

MARIA This could be the fevers.

TOM Maria, look . . .

MARIA Where?

TOM *Here.* Look *here.* If I die, tell them this.

MARIA We all will die, sinhors—God willing.

TOM Last night I ate supper at the hotel.

MARIA The food was good?

TOM *Eugh.*

MARIA I am told it is good.

TOM Middle of the night I thought I was going to die.

MARIA You know I think this every day, but here I am. God willing.

TOM Maria.

MARIA Si.

TOM I don't want Dr. Fritz anymore.

MARIA No?

TOM No. I just want to die.

MARIA No, no, no, no, sinhors. Don't you see, the world are a great battle between the forces of the light, and the forces of the darkness. You must always stay on the side of the forces of light.

TOM Look . . . Please don't say where.

MARIA I love you, Tom.

TOM You what?

MARIA Do you love me?

TOM   No.

MARIA   This is the unrequited love. No?

TOM   Si.

MARIA   God love you too.

TOM   I need a doctor!

RING.

MARIA (*picks up the doll and speaks into it*)   Bonjour. Si. Si. Si. Si. No. Ciao. (*hangs up*) This was God. He say you should believe in him.

TOM   Where is he?

MARIA   God? Upstairs.

TOM   Dr. Fritz. *Can I talk to Dr. Fritz? Please?*

MARIA   Of course you can talk to Dr. Fritz.

TOM   Okay. So where is he?

MARIA   You want to make an appointment?

TOM   I'm getting out of here. (*starts out, but is stopped by pain*) Eugh.

MARIA   Ah, but where will you go, sinhors? And how will you get there in your present conditions?

Tom sinks down and lies on the floor.

TOM   So this is where I'm going to die. I'm going to die here, I'm going to die here, I'm going to die—!

MARIA/DR. FRITZ   *Stille! Stille, du elender Hund! Du rückenloses Tier!* ("Quiet! You miserable dog! You spineless beast!")

TOM   What . . . ?

MARIA/DR. FRITZ   *Halt's Maul, du verfluchter Wurm! Oder sterben Sie! Na gut! Sterben Sie mal! Was geht das mich an?* ("Shut up, you

40

confounded worm! Or else die! Go ahead! Die! What does it matter to me?")

TOM What's going on here . . . ?

MARIA/DR. FRITZ (*German accent*) "I am dying, I am dying!" Ja, ja, perhaps you are dying. If I can shtop this dying I vill shtop it. I am not a magician. I am a physician. But you must listen, ja? You are listening? Ja?

TOM Ja.

MARIA/DR. FRITZ Ja?

TOM Ja.

MARIA/DR. FRITZ *Gut.* I am Dr. Fritz Ringsvwant'l. How do you do.

TOM Dr. Rings . . .

MARIA/DR. FRITZ Vwant'l.

TOM Vandel.

MARIA/DR. FRITZ Vwant'l.

TOM Vandel.

MARIA/DR. FRITZ Dr. Fritz. Okay?

TOM This is definitely fever . . .

MARIA/DR. FRITZ *Also. Auf geht's.* ("So. Get up.")

TOM What?

MARIA/DR. FRITZ Shtand up on your footses.

TOM I—I can't . . .

MARIA/DR. FRITZ *AUF GEHT'S, DU FAULER SCHWEIN! LOS! LOS!* ("Get up, you lazy pig! Move! Move!" *Tom gets up.*) "I can't get up!" You people. Too many Coca-Colas, it has eaten your brains. You haff no will anymore. Too much of ze French fries mit ketchup at ze Golden Arches von McDonald's.

TOM Can I sit in the chair?

MARIA/DR. FRITZ Ziss is Dr. Fritz's chairs. Only Dr. Fritz can sit in ziss chairs. You—on the table zitzen. *Schnell! Schnell!* ("Fast! Fast!" *Tom sits on the table edge. Dr. Fritz takes out a pair of pliers.*) Na gut. Open vide.

TOM Open wide?

MARIA/DR. FRITZ You haff ze troothache?

TOM No.

MARIA/DR. FRITZ *Vas?* I hear zere vas a man mit ze troothache.

TOM That's Pablo. I'm Tom.

MARIA/DR. FRITZ Who you are is not important, you mindless amoeba. (*looks in each of Tom's eyes quickly*) Zo. You haff ze conztipation zometimes, ja?

TOM I do have the constipation sometimes.

MARIA/DR. FRITZ Und zometimes maybe you get a little prickly shtinging pain just behind ze Ellenbogen, hier, hmm? ("*Ellenbogen*" *is* "*elbow.*")

TOM I do get a little prickly pain right there.

MARIA/DR. FRITZ Und you haff ze very ugly dandruff.

TOM I do have dandruff.

MARIA/DR. FRITZ Zo I zee. You must use Head und Shoulders.

TOM I do use Head and Shoulders.

MARIA/DR. FRITZ Vunce a day, or tvice a day?

TOM Once.

MARIA/DR. FRITZ You must use this tvice a day and make ze good bubbly lather, ja? *Deine Hand.*

TOM What?

MARIA/DR. FRITZ Giff me your hand! *Schnell!* (*takes Tom's hand and feels the pulse*) Your pulse is normal.

TOM You're not wearing a watch.

MARIA/DR. FRITZ Your eyesight is excellent. Open your mouth. Stick out your tongue. Go like this.

He makes a raspberry. Tom does too.

No, like this.

Another raspberry. Tom does too.

Better. Now put your fingers in your ears. Can you hear me?

TOM What?

MARIA/DR. FRITZ Good. (*slaps him on the top of the head*)

TOM Ow!

MARIA/DR. FRITZ This hurts?

TOM Yes it hurts.

MARIA/DR. FRITZ A good sign. (*takes out an ancient stethoscope*) Lift ze blouse.

TOM Aren't you going to take my temperature?

MARIA/DR. FRITZ Ziss is a poor country, Meine Herren. I haff nothing here! Nothing! (*feels Tom's forehead quickly*) Besides— you haff no fever.

TOM But I'm shaking!

MARIA/DR. FRITZ Ziss is not fever. Ziss is shaking. Do you luff me?

TOM No!

MARIA/DR. FRITZ Vhy not?

TOM I don't know you.

MARIA/DR. FRITZ Good answer.

TOM Look—

MARIA/DR. FRITZ (*looking behind*) Vhere?

TOM *Eugh* . . .

MARIA/DR. FRITZ You are sure you haff no troothache!

TOM I DON'T HAVE A GODDAMN TROOTHACHE!

MARIA/DR. FRITZ Just checking. But at four you had ze rheumatic fever. Ja?

TOM I did have rheumatic fever . . .

MARIA/DR. FRITZ At fifteen you had a rash on your butttocks in ze shape of Santa Claus. At twenty you had rhinitis, bronchitis, conjunctivitis, and gonorrhea—a busy year for you. At twenty-two you had ze doppel pneumonia and you thought you were going to die.

TOM I did.

MARIA/DR. FRITZ You died?

TOM I thought I was.

MARIA/DR. FRITZ You know I thought ziss every day myself. Then I did die.

TOM You did?

MARIA/DR. FRITZ I died.

TOM *Died?*

MARIA/DR. FRITZ Did. August, 1916. I was on vacation, I got a pain in my *ough,* kaboom, I am dead.

TOM What was it like?

MARIA/DR. FRITZ I had better days. Now I must vander ze earth to complete my good verks.

TOM Wow.

MARIA/DR. FRITZ Vow indeed. You zleep every day from 12:34 to 7:38 in the morning. You eat usually eggs and toast mit raspberry shmier for breakfast, ze garbage fast food for lunch, maybe ze wiener made from pig balls or a slice of Scheisse you call pizza. At ze nighttimes you eat in a restaurant, sometimes Chinese, sometimes Italian, you haff ze gnocchis mit mushrooms und ze shmall green zalat.

TOM Amazing.

MARIA/DR. FRITZ Eleven forty-two at night you masturbate into a sock. Sometimes the argyle sock, sometimes the tube sock, sometimes the sock mit the clocks on the side.

TOM Good God.

MARIA/DR. FRITZ Ziss is your entire shtupid life.

TOM So what's wrong with me?

MARIA/DR. FRITZ I haff no idea. Lie down. (*Dr. Fritz straps Tom to the table.*)

TOM How do you know all these things about me?

MARIA/DR. FRITZ I am a highly qualified sturgeon.

TOM You know what's funny?

MARIA/DR. FRITZ I am German. Nothing is funny. Ha, ha, ha.

TOM I'm getting a toothache!

MARIA/DR. FRITZ Zympathetic reaction. You vant to buy a zoovenirs?

TOM No.

45

MARIA/DR. FRITZ   Vun of a kinds. (*Maria/Dr. Fritz lays the doll on Tom's sternum.*)

TOM   *OWW!*

MARIA/DR. FRITZ   Your case is not so complicated.

TOM   What's wrong?

MARIA/DR. FRITZ   You need an operation.

TOM   An operation . . . ?

MARIA/DR. FRITZ   Immediately.

TOM   You're kidding. Not here.

MARIA/DR. FRITZ   Here.

TOM   Not in this town.

MARIA/DR. FRITZ   You zee another town?

TOM   Not in this country.

MARIA/DR. FRITZ (*produces some ugly-looking butcher knives*)   Unfortunately, I haff not the proper tools . . .

TOM (*struggling in the bands*)   No. No . . . !

MARIA/DR. FRITZ   I haff no anaesthetic; ziss could be quite painful. (*starts sharpening one of the knives*)

TOM   But I'm fine! I'm fine!

MARIA/DR. FRITZ   Fine? Nein.

TOM   Will you undo these straps, please?

MARIA/DR. FRITZ   The doctor is who, here?

TOM   Who *is* the doctor here?

MARIA/DR. FRITZ (*American accent*)   I'm your mother, Tom. How ya feelin'?

Tom screams.

Does that make you feel better? *Also*—das Messer.

"So—the knife." She approaches Tom with the knife.

TOM   Put that thing down!

MARIA/DR. FRITZ   Perhaps for you ve need ze besser Messer. (*takes out an ENORMOUS KNIFE*)

TOM   I DON'T NEED A MESSER!

MARIA/DR. FRITZ   Okay. You are fine? Then good. (*undoes the straps*) Go. You are free. I am not a torturer, I am a doctor. So go. Go!

Tom gets up, turns and starts to go, but is stopped by a sudden pain that drops him to his knees.

TOM   *Eugh. Eugh.* Oh God . . . !

MARIA/DR. FRITZ   You believe in God?

TOM   Suddenly I feel like total hell.

MARIA/DR. FRITZ   Ja, you don't look too svell.

TOM   I'm getting out of here. (*tries to leave, but stops*)

MARIA/DR. FRITZ   But vhere vill you go? And how vill you get there in ziss conditions?

TOM (*falling to the floor in pain*)   Eugh . . .

MARIA/DR. FRITZ   Do you not realize the place you have come to? The forces arrayed vhich could crush you like a peanut?

Tom whimpers. Thunderclap.

You have finished your good works, I hope.

TOM   No! I haven't done anything! I've eaten hot dogs made from pig balls and I had a rash on my butt and I jerk off into a sock every night.

MARIA/DR. FRITZ   This is not very much. Alas, now ze great battle is joined, Meine Herren, and you are in the middle of the field. Ze forces of light and ze forces of darkness are fighting for you. I only hope zatt you vill find your way to the forces of light very very soon.

TOM   But how?

MARIA/DR. FRITZ   Good kvestion.

RING

Ogh. Ziss doll has been ringing off ze hook all day. (*picks up the doll and speaks into it:*) Pronto. Si. Si. Si. Si. (*to Tom:*) It is for you.

TOM   For me . . . ?

MARIA/DR. FRITZ   Ja. God vants to talk to you.

Tom makes a gesture to say: "I'm not here."

Here. Take it. Be nice. Ziss iss God.

TOM (*takes the doll and speaks into it:*)   Hello . . . ? Yes, this is he . . . Fine. Actually, I'm not feeling so fine, I have a pain in my . . . (*realizing the pain is gone:*) Well, I *thought* I had a pain . . . But you know, it's kind of amazing talking to you like this, so listen, um, God, while I've got you on the line—no, no, no, I understand, you've got other things. I just thought I'd get in a few questions. You know—meaning of life, your general take on things, etcetera. So great. I'll see you later—*much* later. I hope. Nice talking to you. 'Bye. (*puts the doll down*)

MARIA (*Hispanic again, knitting*)   How you are feeling, sinhors? You are feeling better?

TOM   I feel fantastic . . . !

MARIA   That so nice. (*holds up doll*) Souvenirs?

BLACKOUT.

BABEL'S IN ARMS

A desert, represented by a palm tree and a sense of expansive blue sky. A road sign with arrows points in various directions: "NINEVEH 75 mi.," "EGYPT 1,324 mi.," and "EDEN 6 mi.," which has been crossed out. Middle Eastern music. Enter two workers, GORPH and CANNAPHLIT. They wear, respectively, blue and red belted tunics à la 1000 B.C. Primitive tools hang from their belts, and a crowbar from Gorph's belt. They are carrying between them an enormous rectangular building stone, maybe five feet long and two feet high. They inch slowly toward center with it, as . . .

GORPH (*groaning under the stone's weight*) Okay . . . Okay . . . Okay . . .

CANNAPHLIT Okay?

GORPH Okay.

CANNAPHLIT Okay?

GORPH Okay. Okay. Okay. Okay. Stop.

A moment, as they catch their breath.

CANNAPHLIT Okay?

GORPH Go.

BOTH (*ad lib, moving toward center*) Okay. Okay. Okay. Okay. Okay. Okay. Okay. Okay. Okay. Okay.

GORPH Stop.

They catch their breath a moment.

Go.

They move a few inches.

Stop.

They stop to catch their breath, but this time they insouciantly hold the stone with just a finger or two, making it obvious it's just a Styrofoam prop.

Go.

Immediately:

Stop.

A moment.

Go.

CANNAPHLIT (*at center now*)   Stop.

GORPH   Okay. Down.

They slowly lower the stone.

Down. Down. Down. Down. Down. Stop. (*looks at it.*) Behold. The fucker is backwards.

They go in a circle.

Circle.

CANNAPHLIT   Circle.

GORPH   Circle.

CANNAPHLIT   Circle.

GORPH   Circle.

CANNAPHLIT   Circle.

GORPH   Stop.

The back looks just like the front. They check position.

It was right the first way. Circle.

They circle back the other way.

CANNAPHLIT   Circle.

GORPH   Circle.

CANNAPHLIT   Circle.

GORPH   Circle.

CANNAPHLIT Circle.

GORPH Circle. Stop.

A moment.

CANNAPHLIT Okay?

GORPH Okay. Down.

CANNAPHLIT Down.

GORPH Down.

CANNAPHLIT Down.

GORPH Up.

CANNAPHLIT Down.

GORPH Up, up.

CANNAPHLIT Up.

GORPH Up.

CANNAPHLIT Up.

A pause.

GORPH Down . . . Down . . . Down . . . Down . . . Stop.

They now have it an inch over the ground.

One. Two. Five. Go!

They drop the stone to the ground.

Behold the stone.

CANNAPHLIT Behold the stone!

BOTH Yes!

They snort, they high-five, they shake hands, they flex their muscles, they grab crotch, and generally male-display.

GORPH   Heavy.

CANNAPHLIT   Heavy.

They moan, they groan, they stretch, they wipe sweat from their foreheads.

GORPH   Heavy stone.

CANNAPHLIT   Heavy stone.

GORPH   Big stone.

CANNAPHLIT   Big stone.

They moan, they groan, they stretch, they wipe sweat from each other's foreheads.

But what is a "stone," O Gorph son of Khlekhmalekhm?

GORPH   That heavy fucker there. That is a stone, O Cannaphlit son of Bob.

CANNAPHLIT   Ah, so that is a stone.

GORPH   Behold the stone!

CANNAPHLIT   Behold the stone! But are all similar fuckers whatever their size or color called a "stone"?

GORPH   Any fucker made of stone is called a "stone."

CANNAPHLIT   But is this stone in the right place, O Gorph son of Khlekhmalekhm?

GORPH   I will consult the plans, O Cannaphlit son of Bob. (*He takes out a large parchment roll.*) Behold the plans.

CANNAPHLIT   Behold the plans!

Gorph unrolls a blueprint—a large blue sheet of paper with just a single white rectangle in the middle.

GORPH   It looks close to me. Check the horizon.

CANNAPHLIT   Check the horizon. (*Cannaphlit pats his pockets.*) What's a horizon?

GORPH (*pointing over audience*)   Behold the horizon.

CANNAPHLIT   Behold the horizon! (*Cannaphlit puts up his hands to his eyes as if he were holding binoculars and scans the horizon.*)

GORPH   But why do you hold your hands in that silly-ass way, O son of Bob?

CANNAPHLIT   Because binoculars have not been invented yet.

GORPH   And what do you see on the horizon?

CANNAPHLIT   I see nothing.

GORPH   Not Nineveh?

CANNAPHLIT   Negative.

GORPH   Accad?

CANNAPHLIT   Eh–eh.

GORPH   Sodom?

CANNAPHLIT   Nada'm.

GORPH   Rehoboth-Ur?

CANNAPHLIT   No thur.

GORPH   The stone must move one sixteenth of an ell to the north!

CANNAPHLIT   One sixteenth of an ell! How far is that?

GORPH   About an inch.

CANNAPHLIT (*as Gorph takes out the crowbar*)   What is that fucker, O my friend?

GORPH   This fucker has no name, for humanity is young and has not words yet for every fucker. Basically it's a rigid rod that pivots about a fulcrum and is used to move an object at point A by applying force at point B.

CANNAPHLIT   Oh.

GORPH   I call it a lever.

CANNAPHLIT   Oh, so that's a lever.

GORPH   Behold young levers wherever you are.

CANNAPHLIT   Behold the lever!

GORPH   I think humanity's had enough of that locution.

CANNAPHLIT   I will can it.

GORPH   Can it, O Cannaphlit. (*With a huge grunt, he levers the stone an inch to the left; that done, he checks, and nudges it with his toe one last small bit.*) The stone is now in place.

CANNAPHLIT   The stone is in place!

They snort, high-five, shake hands, flex muscles, grab crotch, and generally male-display.

So what is the stone for, O Gorph?

GORPH   This stone? This stone is for . . . I do not know. You mean thou dost not know?

CANNAPHLIT   I dost not know.

They regard the stone a moment.

GORPH   Prob'ly some dost-belt development.

CANNAPHLIT   Maybe condos.

A EUNUCH *enters.*

EUNUCH (*very high falsetto*)   Make way! Make way for the high priestess of Shinar!

GORPH   Eunuch?

CANNAPHLIT   Eunuch.

The Eunuch blows a toy trumpet, leading a procession: a BUSINESSWOMAN *in a killer suit with a large sword in a scabbard,* and a PRIESTESS *in outrageous outfit and very high platform shoes, who makes curious gestures. The businesswoman sets up a sign that says "FUTURE HOME OF BABEL."*

GORPH Did I say development? "Future home of Baybel."

BUSINESSWOMAN Babble.

GORPH Excuse me?

BUSINESSWOMAN It's not "Baybel." It's Babble.

GORPH Oh. Babble not Baybel.

CANNAPHLIT I can't even read, but it's spelled "Baybel."

BUSINESSWOMAN Well it's Babble—rabble.

CANNAPHLIT Okay, fine.

GORPH The birth of the class structure. You were there.

PRIESTESS (*blessing the stone*) Oh wow. Oh wow. Oh wow. Oh wow.

CANNAPHLIT High priestess?

GORPH Sure looks high to me.

PRIESTESS In the name of Nimrod, omnipotent and immortal king of the land of Shinar!

EUNUCH (*bringing a potato on a velvet cushion; high falsetto*) Behold the sacred potato!

GORPH & CANNAPHLIT (*falsetto, mocking him*) Behold the sacred potato!

EUNUCH (*aside to them, not in falsetto*) Eat me, okay? This is my *job*.

PRIESTESS (*shaking the potato over the stone*) In the name of the sacred potato, I hereby consecrate this tower . . . (*realizes it's only a stone*) I consecrate this future tower of Baybel . . . Is it "Baybel" or "Babble"?

57

BUSINESSWOMAN Babble.

PRIESTESS It's spelled like Baybel.

BUSINESSWOMAN The CEO says "Babble."

PRIESTESS Okay, so . . . (*shakes sacred potato again*) . . . Babble . . . district of Ammalekhkh, county of Cush, state of blah blah blah, to the greater power and glory of our mighty king Nimrod and his wife Debbie. All say "Oh wow."

ALL Oh wow.

PRIESTESS Amen.

CANNAPHLIT I found that service quite moving.

GORPH The pomp.

CANNAPHLIT The solemnity.

GORPH The tradition.

BUSINESSWOMAN (*to High Priestess*) Listen, thanks for doing this, Your Priestess. If I could make a small gift to the spiritual sector . . .

PRIESTESS God is grateful for any contribution, no matter how small.

Businesswoman slips her a small sack of gold.

How small is it?

BUSINESSWOMAN Fifty schmootzkels.

PRIESTESS Fifty schmootzkels? You brought me out here for fifty schmootzkels?

BUSINESSWOMAN (*another small sack*) Seventy-five schmootzkels.

PRIESTESS The potato ceremony with music and castrato for seventy-five schmootzkels? Plus it's hot out here, I missed a luncheon with a sorcerer, I hadda wear these fucking *shoes* . . .

BUSINESSWOMAN (*another small sack*) A hundred schmootzkels, Your Priestess.

PRIESTESS Bless you, my child. Eunuch, the music!

The Eunuch blows on the toy trumpet as the two head out, the priestess blessing all:

Oh wow . . . Oh wow . . . Oh wow . . .

The Eunuch and Priestess exit.

BUSINESSWOMAN Now listen up, you rotten stinking men.

GORPH Things would be so much better under a patriarchy.

CANNAPHLIT Kinder. Gentler.

BUSINESSWOMAN I represent a consortium of off-desert investors who want to develop this property. Our mandate is to build a tower whose top will reach to the very heavens, indeed, into heaven, indeed, as high as God. Indeed, meeting God.

GORPH Heavy.

CANNAPHLIT Indeed heavy.

BUSINESSWOMAN This in order to show that we are equal to same aforesaid God.

GORPH That we are equal to God?

BUSINESSWOMAN No, that *we,* not you, are equal to same aforesaid God. You are nothing. You are scum, you are excrement, but you build the tower. Have you got that?

GORPH We're scum.

CANNAPHLIT We're excrement.

GORPH We build the tower.

BUSINESSWOMAN In the event that same aforesaid God is not pleased, the consortium is not responsible for any long-term apocalyptic events. Sign here. (*presents a parchment; immediately takes it away*) Understood. Now. The most important thing. And this is absolutely crucial. Are you listening?

They nod.

Do not—under any circumstances—khlumnafluffa himnaflekh.

GORPH Excuse me?

BUSINESSWOMAN Do NOT . . . khlumnafluffa himnaflekh.

GORPH Oh, right. Right . . . Khlumnafluffa . . .

CANNAPHLIT Do not khlumnafluffa bimbaflekh.

BUSINESSWOMAN Himmm-naflekh.

CANNAPHLIT Himmmmm-naflekh.

BUSINESSWOMAN (*pulls sword from its scabbard*) Or else you die. Instructions clear?

BOTH Mm-hm . . . Oh yeah . . . I think so . . . Very clear . . .

BUSINESSWOMAN One last crucial thing. Do you have the shpoont?

GORPH The what?

BUSINESSWOMAN The shpoont. Did you bring the shpoont?

GORPH Oh, the *shpoont*.

CANNAPHLIT I think we have the shpoont.

GORPH The shpoont was here a moment ago.

BUSINESSWOMAN Do not proceed without the shpoont. (*takes out the sword*) Or else you die.

GORPH We will use the shpoont!

CANNAPHLIT Use the shpoont! How's the pay on this job?

BUSINESSWOMAN Your lives.

CANNAPHLIT Good pay.

BUSINESSWOMAN I'll be checking in very soon.

GORPH Anytime. Please.

BUSINESSWOMAN Now get to work.

GORPH Forthwith.

CANNAPHLIT Thank you.

GORPH Goodbye!

CANNAPHLIT See you!

GORPH Ciao!

Businesswoman exits.

Khlumnafluffa himnaflekh . . .

CANNAPHLIT Khlumnafluffa himnaflekh. . . .

GORPH What the heyyyyy is that?

CANNAPHLIT That was a little vague. The other instructions were
pretty clear.

GORPH Oh yes? Repeat the instructions. Refresh my memory.

CANNAPHLIT Build a tower whose top reaches to the very
heavens, indeed, into heaven, indeed as high as God.

GORPH Indeed meeting God.

CANNAPHLIT Indeed meeting God. Proving that they—not we
because we are excrement—that they are equal to same aforesaid
God.

GORPH That's very clear.

CANNAPHLIT And don't khlumnafluffa himnaflekh, or you die.

GORPH And don't forget the shpoont.

CANNAPHLIT   The shpoont was mysterious.

GORPH   The shpoont was *crystalline,* compared to the God part.

CANNAPHLIT   Maybe we could put a portico on the tower, in pink, do a rich pink ceiling, maybe use that sponging technique . . .

GORPH   But consider this, O son of Bob. Putting the pink portico aside for a moment. How high do you think we have to go, to meet, say, "God"?

CANNAPHLIT   Whoo. Well. God, huh . . . I'd say high.

GORPH   High?

CANNAPHLIT   Pretty high.

GORPH   Pretty high. Several ells high?

CANNAPHLIT   Maybe higher.

GORPH   How about mighty high?

CANNAPHLIT   Mighty high. Measuring could be a problem.

GORPH   Mm-hm. And let us nail down why. Name an attribute of God. Go ahead. Just pick an attribute, any attribute.

CANNAPHLIT   Well . . . God has two arms and two legs.

GORPH   Obviously.

CANNAPHLIT   Hair like us.

GORPH   Hair like us.

CANNAPHLIT   God is fairly powerful.

GORPH   Powerful. Mm-hmm . . .

CANNAPHLIT   God wears little red belted fuckers like this one.

GORPH   We'll let that pass. Any other attributes?

CANNAPHLIT   I'd say God is eternal and infinite.

GORPH   Infinite. Let's pause there for a nanosecond. How high would a tower have to be to meet an infinite God?

CANNAPHLIT   Hmmm. (*He ponders that a moment, then raises his hand like a student.*)

GORPH (*teacher*)   Cannaphlit.

CANNAPHLIT   Infinitely high?

GORPH   Infinitely high. So you're going infinitely high—how broad would the base of same aforesaid tower would have to be? Just gimme a rough guesstimate. (*Pause as Cannaphlit ponders that. Then he raises his hand again like a student. Teacher:*) Cannaphlit.

CANNAPHLIT   Infinitely broad?

GORPH   Innnnfinitely broad. How many stones would we have to use, us two assholes, to build this infinite tower?

CANNAPHLIT   Well . . .

GORPH   An *innnnnnfinite* number of stones. And how long did it take us to get this stone here?

CANNAPHLIT   Two years.

GORPH   So our task, just to clarify, is to build a tower infinitely high, infinitely broad, from an infinite number of stones, shake hands with God AND—do not khlumnafluffa himnaflekh while using the shpoont.

CANNAPHLIT   It's gonna be work.

GORPH   It's gonna be work.

CANNAPHLIT (*brilliant idea*)   Maybe we should get out of it!

GORPH   But how, O brilliant Son of Bob?

They sit on the stone and ponder, straining audibly as if on the toilet.

CANNAPHLIT   We could refuse.

GORPH Sit-down strike. Organize the workers.

CANNAPHLIT We *are* the workers.

GORPH So we're organized already.

CANNAPHLIT Why should we get sucked into some pyramid scheme?

GORPH Millennium fever, that's what I call it.

CANNAPHLIT This tower isn't set in stone. Well, not yet—

GORPH Not ever!

CANNAPHLIT Not ever!

GORPH We just say no. But we need a reason. So when they ask us why we've laid down our fuckers, we say . . . ?

They sit and ponder again, straining at stool more loudly.

CANNAPHLIT We could tell them God doesn't exist.

GORPH I love it.

CANNAPHLIT No God—no tower.

GORPH It's simple. It's elegant.

CANNAPHLIT What can they do?

GORPH Cut off our heads?

They ponder again, straining more loudly still.

CANNAPHLIT Wait a minute. Who says God is in the sky?

GORPH Yeah! Where did this arcane idea come from?

CANNAPHLIT Maybe God isn't up, maybe God is *down*.

GORPH Oh, man, it's brilliant. Brilliant!

CANNAPHLIT We don't have to build a tower infinitely high and infinitely broad! We just have to dig a big hole!

They celebrate, but then realize:

BOTH (*variously*)   An infinite hole . . .

GORPH   Infinitely deep.

CANNAPHLIT   Infinitely wide.

GORPH   Infinitely . . . infinite.

Pause.

CANNAPHLIT   Where do you put the dirt?

GORPH   Big engineering problem.

CANNAPHLIT   Major engineering problem. Speaking of which, the stone is off.

GORPH   It's what?

CANNAPHLIT   It's not level. Give me the thing.

GORPH   The "thing"? What's a "thing"?

CANNAPHLIT   The fucker.

GORPH   Oh, you mean the fucker.

CANNAPHLIT   Yeah. The leever.

GORPH   You mean the lever?

CANNAPHLIT   I say leever, you say lever, I claim the whole thing's off!

GORPH   What, you mean the stone isn't *leevel*? I suppose you also say "potahto."

CANNAPHLIT   No, I say "potayto."

GORPH   Well where I come from I say "potayto." So you can't. And I'll tell you another thing. Shmoloch does not wear little red belted fuckers like that, Shmoloch wears blue belted fuckers like this.

CANNAPHLIT (*nose to nose*)   Oh yeah? Who's Shmoloch?

GORPH   Shmoloch the great and omnipotent creator of the universe.

CANNAPHLIT   God's name is not Shmoloch. It's Houlihan.

GORPH   Houlihan?

CANNAPHLIT   The magnificent. And Houlihan wears little red belted fuckers like this.

GORPH   It's Shmoloch, in blue.

CANNAPHLIT   Houlihan, in red.

GORPH   How do you know?

CANNAPHLIT   I've seen the hieroglyphs.

GORPH (*drawing a line in the sand*)   Cross this line, I dare you.

CANNAPHLIT (*drawing another*)   No, you cross *this* line!

GORPH   No, no, no, you cross *my* line!

CANNAPHLIT   What's a line?

GORPH   That fucker right there, that's a line. And it's innnnfinite, it's infinitely long, so just try.

CANNAPHLIT   Wait a minute. (*tapping his head with a brilliant idea*) Candlepower! Candlepower!

GORPH   What've you got? What. What. What.

CANNAPHLIT   We tell them God is everywhere. If God is everywhere, you don't have to build a tower or dig a hole or nothin'!

GORPH   Because we're already *there*.

They celebrate wildly for a moment, then stop suddenly.

   Is it true?

66

CANNAPHLIT I don't know. We could *say* it.

They go back to celebrating.

BOTH Whoo–EEEEE!

CANNAPHLIT We're there, buddy!

GORPH We did it!

They snort, high-five, shake hands, flex their muscles, grab their crotches, and generally male-display. The Businesswoman comes in and watches them celebrate.

BUSINESSWOMAN So how are we doing?

BOTH Good. Good. We're doing good. Excellent.

GORPH Look not an ell farther.

CANNAPHLIT There it is.

GORPH (*arms wide over the audience*) Behold!

CANNAPHLIT (*arms wide over the audience*) The tower!

A pause.

BUSINESSWOMAN Excuse me?

GORPH Behold!

CANNAPHLIT The tower!

GORPH Shake hands with God, baby. 'Cause we are DONE.

BUSINESSWOMAN (*draws the sword*) Explain this to my trusty sword.

CANNAPHLIT Well . . . You don't need a tower because God is everywhere. You see?

BUSINESSWOMAN I see nothing. And my sword sees nothing.

CANNAPHLIT Maybe you're not looking hard enough. (*points*) God is here. (*points elsewhere*) God is here.

GORPH God is here.

CANNAPHLIT God's over there.

GORPH God is this.

CANNAPHLIT God is that.

GORPH God's up there, God's down there.

They keep this up as the Businesswoman maintains her blank expression. Gradually they run out of steam:

CANNAPHLIT And God is there . . .

GORPH And God is there . . .

CANNAPHLIT And here . . .

GORPH I swear to God. Who is everywhere. As you see.

Silence.

BUSINESSWOMAN Did you khlumnafluffa himnaflekh?

BOTH (*ad lib*) Oh no. No, no. Uh-uh. Never. Not at all. Mm-mm. Didn't think of it. Nope. No way.

BUSINESSWOMAN Did you use the shpoont?

GORPH *Constantly.*

BUSINESSWOMAN I don't believe you. Prepare to die. (*She raises the sword.*)

CANNAPHLIT *We saved your life!*

BUSINESSWOMAN I beg your pardon?

CANNAPHLIT The tower you wanted would've taken an innnnnfinite number of stones which would've cost an innnnnfinite number of schmootzkels. Consortium calls you in— you're cold cuts, babe. Or Bab.

The Businesswoman considers that a moment.

BUSINESSWOMAN   Gentlemen—I LOVE THIS TOWER.

CANNAPHLIT   Pretty nice, huh.

BUSINESSWOMAN   It's beautiful! It's got balance, it's got harmony.

GORPH   Put together an infinite number of nothing—eventually, you get this.

CANNAPHLIT   How do you like the portico?

BUSINESSWOMAN   The portico is my favorite part! Where did you find that pink?

CANNAPHLIT (*to Gorph*)   Did I say pink portico?

BUSINESSWOMAN   Congratulations!

Now all three of them snort, flex, shake hands, etc.

Well you guys did a terrific job and the consortium thanks you. So as a bonus here's a bag of cow manure for you.

The Eunuch enters and gives a dripping bag to Gorph, and another to Cannaphlit.

And a bag of cow manure for you.

GORPH   Golly. Thanks a lot. That's cow manure all right.

CANNAPHLIT   Nice and fresh too.

BUSINESSWOMAN   As an option you could be castrated and be sacred eunuchs.

BOTH (*ad lib*)   Oh, that's all right . . . I think the cow manure is enough . . .

BUSINESSWOMAN   We won't forget this. Thank you.

CANNAPHLIT   Our pleasure.

BUSINESSWOMAN   Don't spread that all in one place.

GORPH   You're a caution. You're a card.

Businesswoman exits.

Tower to God, huh. Easier than I thought.

CANNAPHLIT (*pointing to bag of manure*)   That's where thinking'll get you.

GORPH   And it's Shmoloch, in blue.

CANNAPHLIT   Houlihan, in red.

GORPH   Blue.

CANNAPHLIT   Red.

GORPH   Blue.

A loud thundercrack. They grovel, daven, and make conciliatory signs.

So listen. Now we found God—you wanna invent the wheel?

CANNAPHLIT   Yeah. What's a wheel?

GORPH   I dunno. We'll fake it.

GORPH & CANNAPHLIT   YES!

BLACKOUT.

ARABIAN NIGHTS

At right, a freestanding, open doorway with a multicolored bead curtain. At center, a small, plain wooden table with a white cloth and a sign that says "SALE." On the table: a picture frame, a stone, a gold ring, and a figure of a frog. at lights up, FLORA—very ordinary—is at the table, dusting the four objects with a featherduster. Through the bead curtain comes NORMAN—utterly normal—who carries a well-traveled suitcase. Immediately, the INTERPRETER appears and leads Norman in. The Interpreter wears loose, colorful robes and sandals, and may be played by a woman wearing a dark beard.

INTERPRETER   Right this way, sir, this way. The most beautiful shop in the world. All the wonders of the kingdom. For nothing! Nothing!

NORMAN (*to Flora, tongue-tied*)   Ehhhhh . . .

INTERPRETER   Ehhhhh . . . I will interpret for you.

NORMAN   Hello.

INTERPRETER   Hail, fair maid! says he.

FLORA (*to Norman, putting the featherduster away*)   Good morning.

INTERPRETER   All praise to the highest, says she.

NORMAN   Do you . . . um . . . speak any English?

INTERPRETER   Do you . . . um . . . speak any English?

FLORA (*She speaks perfect, unaccented English.*)   Yes, I speak some English.

INTERPRETER   Indeed, sir, I can stammer out a broken song of pitiful, insufficient words.

NORMAN   Ah-ha.

INTERPRETER   Ah-ha.

NORMAN   Well . . .

INTERPRETER   A deep hole in the ground.

NORMAN I . . .

INTERPRETER (*points to his eye*) The organ of vision.

NORMAN Ummm . . .

INTERPRETER Ummm . . .

NORMAN Listen.

INTERPRETER Do you hear something?

They all listen for something.

NORMAN I'm sorry to rush in so late like this.

INTERPRETER I'm sorry to rush in so late like this.

FLORA No, please.

INTERPRETER No, please.

NORMAN But you see . . .

INTERPRETER (*points to his butt*) But—(*points to* FLORA)—*you*—(*does binoculars with his hands*)—see . . .

NORMAN (*looks at his watch*) Darn it, it's late . . .

INTERPRETER (*produces an hourglass*) How swiftly flow the sands of time!

NORMAN I know this sounds crazy—

INTERPRETER Am I insane? Give me an opinion.

NORMAN I only have about ten minutes.

INTERPRETER Soon the shining orb of heaven will cleave the house of the hedgehog.

NORMAN I have to catch a plane.

INTERPRETER I must clamber upon the flying corporate carpet and flap away from your kingdom.

NORMAN Anyway, I want to find . . .

INTERPRETER Anyway, I want to find . . .

FLORA Yes?

INTERPRETER Yes?

NORMAN I guess you'd call it . . .

INTERPRETER Something unparalleled! Something sublime!

NORMAN A souvenir.

INTERPRETER (*You're kidding.*) A *souvenir* . . . ?!

NORMAN Something to take with me.

INTERPRETER A treasure!

FLORA Any particular kind of thing?

INTERPRETER Can the funicular hide the spring?

NORMAN Excuse me?

INTERPRETER Accuse me?

FLORA How much did you want to spend?

INTERPRETER How much did you want to spend?

NORMAN It doesn't matter.

INTERPRETER Let's haggle. I'm loaded!

FLORA Is this for yourself?

INTERPRETER Have you a mistress, a wife, a *hareem*?

NORMAN No, this is for me.

INTERPRETER Alas and alack, a lad alone in all the world am I. La la la!

FLORA Well . . .

INTERPRETER   A deep hole in the ground.

FLORA   I think I can help you.

INTERPRETER   Solitary sir, the maiden says, I look in your eyes and I see your soul shining there like a golden carp in an azure pool.

NORMAN   Really . . . ?

INTERPRETER   Really. Now, in this brief moment, in the midst of this mirage called life, here on this tiny square of soil on the whirling earth, I feel the two of us joined by a crystal thread, your soul to my soul to yours.

NORMAN   You do?

INTERPRETER   You do?

FLORA   I do.

INTERPRETER   She does.

NORMAN   You know, I've been up and down this street every day . . .

INTERPRETER   Day and night have I shlepped through the kasbah . . .

NORMAN   I sure wish I'd seen this shop sooner.

INTERPRETER   . . . only so that I might glimpse you.

FLORA   I've noticed you walking by.

INTERPRETER   How I pined for you to enter as you passed.

NORMAN   You did?

INTERPRETER   She did. She asks your name.

NORMAN   My name is Norman.

INTERPRETER   My name is Sinbad!

NORMAN   I'm here on some business.

INTERPRETER   I am the merchant son of a great prince, exiled from my land.

FLORA   Is that so.

INTERPRETER   Her name is Izthatso.

NORMAN   Is that so?

FLORA   People call me Flora.

INTERPRETER   But people call me Flora.

FLORA   With an "F."

INTERPRETER   With an "F." Of course.

NORMAN   I . . .

INTERPRETER   The organ of vision.

NORMAN (*looks at watch*)   Darn it . . .

INTERPRETER (*produces hourglass*)   Darn it . . .

NORMAN   Y'know, Flora . . .

INTERPRETER   Y'know, Flora . . .

NORMAN   You shop and you shop . . .

INTERPRETER   We live our brief and miserable lives . . .

NORMAN   . . . you never seem to find that special thing you're shopping for.

INTERPRETER   . . . each day awaiting the donut of happiness.

FLORA   That's so true.

INTERPRETER   That's so true.

NORMAN   Maybe what I'm looking for is right here.

INTERPRETER   Perhaps today my donut has dawned.

FLORA   Shhh!

INTERPRETER Shhh!

FLORA I thought I heard my father.

INTERPRETER My father may be listening!

FLORA It's almost time for his tea.

INTERPRETER If he sees me talking to you, he'll cut your throat!

NORMAN & INTERPRETER (*simultaneous as they pick up the suitcase together*) Maybe I should be going . . .

FLORA No—

INTERPRETER For God's sake!

FLORA He won't bother us.

INTERPRETER Have mercy, good sir!

NORMAN (*hefts suitcase*) I do have a plane to catch.

INTERPRETER Take my suitcase.

Flora takes the suitcase from him and sets it down.

FLORA There's plenty of time.

INTERPRETER Keep your voice low.

FLORA Shhh!

INTERPRETER Shhh!

FLORA I thought I heard him calling.

INTERPRETER He's sharpening the blade.

We hear the sound of a blade being sharpened.

NORMAN [*A CRY OF SURPRISE.*]

INTERPRETER [*A CRY OF SURPRISE.*]

FLORA He's just watching old movies.

INTERPRETER   The old man is mad!

FLORA   Anyway, I'm sure I'll have something you'll like.

INTERPRETER   Act as if you're buying something.

NORMAN   What about these things right here?

INTERPRETER   What about these things right here?

FLORA   Maybe you'd like a picture frame?

INTERPRETER   Can you conceive, prince, how lonely my days are? They are as empty as a silver frame awaiting a picture.

FLORA   Or maybe a stone?

INTERPRETER   My life is as hard—and as cheap—as this stone.

FLORA (*gestures left*)   I have more in the back.

INTERPRETER (*gestures left*)   He keeps me locked in a tiny cell at the back.

NORMAN   No. No.

INTERPRETER   Stay with me.

FLORA   Maybe you'd like . . .

INTERPRETER   What I truly long for . . .

FLORA   . . . a golden ring?

INTERPRETER   . . . is love. The endless golden donut of love.

FLORA   If not a ring, maybe a figurine?

INTERPRETER   But my father has betrothed me to a man as ugly as this frog.

FLORA   Does that interest you?

INTERPRETER   Would you marry this?

NORMAN   Not really.

INTERPRETER Not really.

FLORA I don't know what else I can show you.

INTERPRETER I have nothing, sir. Nichts! Nada! Niente!

NORMAN My God, you're beautiful.

INTERPRETER My God, you're beautiful.

FLORA Excuse me?

INTERPRETER Beh, beh, beh, what?

NORMAN I'm sorry.

INTERPRETER I'm not sorry I said it.

NORMAN I don't usually say things like that.

INTERPRETER Though I know I sound like a jerk.

NORMAN You know, sometimes it's something so simple.

INTERPRETER So complicated are the ways of kismet.

NORMAN You walk into a shop . . .

INTERPRETER I look at you . . .

NORMAN . . . and everything's suddenly different, somehow.

INTERPRETER . . . and my heart flutters inside me like a leaf of the perfumed gum tree at the scented bounce of bedspring.

FLORA Really?

INTERPRETER Really.

NORMAN Now in this brief moment . . .

INTERPRETER Now in this brief moment . . .

NORMAN . . . on this tiny patch of ground on the whirling earth . . .

INTERPRETER . . . in the midst of this mirage called life . . .

NORMAN . . . I feel us joined by a crystal thread, your soul to my soul to yours.

INTERPRETER Etcetera, etcetera, etcetera.

FLORA You do?

INTERPRETER You do?

NORMAN I . . .

INTERPRETER The organ of vision.

NORMAN . . . do.

INTERPRETER He does.

NORMAN How can I leave, now that I've seen you, met you, heard you?

INTERPRETER How can I get on a plane and eat that food?

NORMAN Now that fate has brought me to this bazaar?

INTERPRETER It's so bizarre.

NORMAN (*takes out an hourglass*) O cruel fate! How swiftly flow the sands of time!

INTERPRETER (*looks at a watch*) O shit, I gotta get outa here . . . !

NORMAN The stars have decreed we must part. (*He kisses Flora's hand.*) But I will return, O my florid queen!

INTERPRETER Maybe I'll pass this way again sometime.

FLORA I will wait for you, my Norman prince!

NORMAN O, Izthatso.

FLORA It is so! I will be yours and you will be mine and we will be each other's.

INTERPRETER Hommina hommina hommina, you get the idea.

NORMAN Well . . .

INTERPRETER A deep hole in the ground.

FLORA Well . . .

INTERPRETER With purest spring water at the bottom.

NORMAN Salaam!

INTERPRETER So long!

FLORA Salaam!

INTERPRETER So long! So long! So long!

NORMAN Open, sesame!

Norman whirls out, followed by the Interpreter.

FLORA (*sighs*) Oh, well. (*She takes out the featherduster—and finds that it's been changed into a bouquet of red roses.*) Shazam! (*She starts to dust the objects with the bouquet.*)

BLACKOUT.

ENIGMA VARIATIONS

Two identical chairs, side by side at center left, face two identical chairs side by side at center right. Upstage, two adjoining windows look out on exactly the same cityscape. A bell rings, and lights come up on BILL 1 *standing at far left,* BEBE 1 *at far right. Bill 1 wears a white lab coat and glasses, Bebe 1 an attractive but demure outfit.*

BILL 1 Good morning, good morning. Ms. Doppelgängler?

BEBE 1 Actually, *Mrs.* Doppelgängler. Bebe W. W. Doppelgängler. With two small dots.

BILL 1 I'm Bill Williams.

They cross to each other and shake hands, as BILL 2 *and* BEBE 2 *enter just upstage of them and shake hands. Bill 2 and Bebe 2 wear exactly the same clothes as Bill 1 and Bebe 1 and they make every move that their partners make, shadowing every gesture of Bill 1 and Bebe 1.*

BEBE 1 Thank you so much for seeing me, Doctor.

BILL 1 Why don't you call me Bill.

BEBE 1 Bill.

BILL 1 Or Will.

BEBE 1 Will.

BILL 1 Will . . . you have a seat?

BEBE 1 Thank you.

The two Bebes sit and simultaneously adjust their skirts at their knees, as the two Bills sit and in identical fashion adjust their identical glasses.

BILL 1 So. You have been having a problem.

BEBE 1 A couple of problems, you might say. But may we speak alone?

BILL 1 *(looks behind himself)* We are alone.

BEBE 1 *(She and Bebe 2 turn and look over their shoulders.)* Where were we?

BILL 1 We were having a couple of problems.

BEBE 1 I'm not actually sure you're the right person to come to, Doctor.

The Bills make a gesture and she corrects herself:

Bill—Will—Well, you see, lately I've been having this funny feeling that there's more to the world than I thought. Or, think.

BILL 1 Could you . . . expand a little?

BEBE 1 (*She and Bebe 2 take a deep breath, expanding hugely, then letting it out.*) It's as if, when I'm alone in a room, I'm somehow . . . not alone. As if it's not just me there.

BILL 1 Mm-hm, mm-hm.

BEBE 1 And it's not just me. I mean—when I'm with someone it's almost as if there's one more than one of that someone in the room. And as if that one room isn't the only room I'm in. It's as if the world were somehow . . . somehow . . . double.

BILL 1 A singular problem, Mrs. Doppelgängler. But you're a singular person. Both of us know that. Two things: you're married?

BEBE 1 I'm single. We split up.

BILL 1 Any siblings?

BEBE 1 My twin sister, in St. Paul.

BILL 1 The twin city. How have you been sleeping?

BEBE 1 I'm up half the night in a double bed.

BILL 1 It doesn't add up.

BEBE 1 I'm desperate, Doctor. Last week I played doubles without a partner.

BILL 1 Did you win?

BEBE I Twice!

BILL I How did you manage that?

BEBE I Duplicity. Doublemint?

BILL I No thank you. Would you read the eye chart, please?

Two identical eye charts fly in, side by side.

BEBE I Which one?

BILL I The one on the left.

BEBE I "E-I-E-I-O."

BILL I And on the right?

BEBE I "E-I-E-I-O."

BILL I Excellent.

The eye charts fly back out.

BEBE I I know this sounds pretty odd.

BILL I Oh, we in my profession hear all kinds of O-D-D-D items.

BEBE I "O-D-D-D" . . . ?

BILL I Odd. But I have news for you, Mrs. Doppelgängler: you are not alone.

BEBE I In what way?

BILL I In two ways.

The Bills rise together and look out the two windows.

Each person, which is to say everybody, looks out at the world and wonders, though apparently there's only one, if there aren't other worlds, and asks if there isn't more to it, or them, than they, that is he or she, think. Or thinks. Maybe, perhaps, there's possibly a higher reality. Or realities. Multiple realities, doing double duty. In any cases, I'm not just Bill W. Williams, and you're not just Bebe—Bebe?—Bebe W. Doppelgängler.

BEBE 1 Bebe W.W. Doppelgängler.

BILL 1 Exactly! And you alone can help yourself.

BEBE 1 If not me, then who?

BILL 1 (*sitting, along with Bill 2*) I stand corrected. The only alternative—ha ha ha!—is that you're crazy. You're not crazy, are you?

BEBE 1 No. No.

BILL 1 Delusional? Mad?

BEBE 1 No . . .

BILL 1 Any—or many—multiple "personalities"?

BEBE 1 No. No. No. No.

The two Bebes take out identical handkerchiefs.

It's as if I'm living some kind of double life. Am I ill, Will?

BILL 1 Well, I think we should see each other again. Possibly again and again. Maybe more than once.

He and Bill 2 press intercom buttons in their chair arms.

Fifi—would you come in here, please?

FIFI *enters, a hairy, burly guy in a nurse's white dress and shoes. He makes no attempt to seem "feminine" or "effeminate."*

FIFI Yes, Doctor. You wanted me?

BILL 1 Bebe—Fifi. Fifi—Bibi. Mademoiselle LeBlanc is my temporary assistant.

FIFI Oui, oui.

BEBE 1 Yes, we, we met.

BILL 1   Fifi, a wee matter. Would you set up a couple of appointments for Mrs. Doppelgängler?

FIFI   Two small dots?

BEBE 1   Two small dots.

BILL 1   I see your points. Same time all right?

BEBE 1   Fine, fine.

BILL 1   Fifi?

FIFI   Oui, oui. (*Fifi exits.*)

BILL 1   A wonderful woman. Dual citizenship. And exclusively bisexual.

BEBE 1   Doctor, can you suggest anything for me?

BILL 1   Maybe, Bebe—a double dose of B1 and B2 taken twice every couple of days for two weeks. As a onetime treatment. Are you covered?

BEBE 1   They pay half. Would you send me a bill, Bill?

BILL 1   In duplicate.

BEBE 1   (*rising, along with Bebe 2*)   Thank you so, so much.

BILL 1   You're very, very welcome.

Bill 1 and Bebe 1 shake hands, Bill 2 and Bebe 2 shake hands. As they do so, they freeze and we hear a bell ring. The scene in the two windows changes to a different cityscape.

BILL 2   Good morning, good morning. Ms. Doppelgängler.

BEBE 2   Actually, *Mrs.* Doppelgängler. Bebe W.W. Doppelgängler.

BILL 2   Two small dots.

BEBE 2   That's right. Thank you so much for seeing me.

BILL 2   Will you have a seat?

The four sit exactly as before.

So. You've been having a recurring problem.

BEBE 2 I have, Doctor.

BILL 2 I *am* Doctor, but you can call me Bill.

BEBE 2 Bill.

BILL 2 Or Will.

BEBE 2 Will.

BILL 2 Well?

BEBE 2 Well, I'm not sure you're the right person to come to, but you see I keep having this feeling . . . I keep having this feeling I've been through all this before.

BILL 2 Could you expand a little?

BEBE 2 (*She and Bebe 1 take deep breaths, expanding hugely, then let them out.*) I feel as if I've been through all this before. It's as if this isn't the first time this has happened to me.

BILL 2 Have we ever been through this before?

BEBE 2 Never.

BILL 2 Have you felt this way often?

BEBE 2 This isn't the first time.

BILL 2 Do your meals repeat on you?

BEBE 2 Again and again. I reiterate.

BILL 2 You reiterate what?

BEBE 2 Nothing, I just keep reiterating.

BILL 2 So your recurring problem is a *recurring* problem.

BEBE 2 Frequently. I even bought a repeating pistol.

BILL 2   Repeating . . . ?

BEBE 2   Repeating pistol.

BILL 2   Will you continue?

BEBE 2   I certainly hope so.

BILL 2   No, I mean—please continue.

BEBE 2   I'm not sure you're the right person to come to, but you see I keep having this feeling . . . I keep having this feeling I've been through this before.

BILL 2   Could you expand a little?

BEBE 2   (*She and Bebe 1 take deep breaths, expanding hugely, then let them out.*) I feel as if I've been through all this before. It's as if this isn't the first time this has happened to me.

BILL 2   Have we ever been through this before?

BEBE 2   Never.

BILL 2   Have you felt this way often?

BEBE 2   This isn't the first time.

BILL 2   Do your meals repeat on you?

BEBE 2   Again and again. I reiterate.

BILL 2   You reiterate what?

BEBE 2   Nothing, I just keep reiterating.

BILL 2   So your recurring problem is a *recurring* problem.

BEBE 2   Frequently. I even bought a repeating pistol.

BILL 2   Repeating . . . ?

BEBE 2   Repeating pistol.

BILL 2   Will you continue?

BEBE 2   I certainly hope so.

BILL 2   No, I mean—please continue.

BEBE 2   I'm not sure you're the right person to come to, Doctor—

BILL 2   Let me say one word. A word I'm sure you've heard before, Mrs. Doppelgängler.

BEBE 2 (*pronounced with a silly, tight "ü"*)   Déjà vuuu?

BILL 2   Déjà vuuu.

BEBE 2   So it's . . . déjà vuuu?

BILL 2   Déjà vuuu. I repeat.

BEBE 2   Déjà vuuu?

BILL 2   Déjà vuuu. Mrs. Doppelgängler, you have a German name but a French disease. I call that serious.

BEBE 2   Well this isn't something I haven't heard before. Déjà vuuu?

BILL 2   Déjà vuuu.

BEBE 2   But this time it really means something.

BILL 2   Ditto.

BEBE 2   But Doctor, what can I, what can I duuu—about deja vuuu?

BILL 2   I think we should see each other again. Possibly again and again. Maybe more than once.

BEBE 2 (*rising, with BEBE 1*)   Thank you so much, Will.

BILL 2   So—come again?

BEBE 2   I said thank you so much, Will.

BILL 2   I mean will you come again.

BEBE 2   I said thank you so much, Will.

BILL 2   No, I mean, will you come here one more time?

BEBE 2   I'd love to.

BILL 2   Just one more time?

BEBE 2   I said I'd love to.

BILL 2   No, I mean will you come . . . ?

BEBE 2   I will, Will.

BILL 2   One more time or many more times?

BEBE 2   How about next week?

BILL 2   Let's reconfirm. Fifi?

Fifi enters.

FIFI   Oui, oui, Doctor.

BILL 2   Repeat the usual.

Fifi exits. Bill 1 shakes hands with Bebe 2 and Bill 2 shakes hands with Bebe 1, and they freeze a moment as a bell rings. The windows change to two totally different scenes.

BEBE 2 [*Gestures as if she's speaking while Bebe 1, remaining very still, speaks for her.*]

BEBE 1   Good morning. How are you, Bill?

BILL 2 [*Gestures as if he's speaking while Bill 1, remaining very still, speaks for him.*]

BILL 1   Thank you for seeing me, Dr. Doppelgängler.

BEBE 2 [*Gestures as before.*]

BEBE 1   That's what we're here for. And please, call me Bebe. Won't you have a seat?

93

BILL 2 [*Gestures as before.*]

The four sit.

BEBE 2 [*Gestures as before.*]

BILL 2 [*Gestures as before.*]

BEBE 2 [*Gestures.*]

BILL 2 [*Gestures.*]

BEBE 2 [*Gestures.*]

BILL 2 [*Gestures.*]

BEBE 2 [*Gestures.*]

BILL 1   Thank you.

BEBE 1   Apparently you seem to be having a possible problem.

BILL 1   Apparently I seem to be having a possible problem. Exactly!

BEBE 1   Could you amplify?

BILL 1 (*very loudly*)   I DON'T KNOW IF YOU'RE THE RIGHT PERSON TO COME TO . . .

BEBE 1   I mean, could you expand a little.

BILL 1 (*breathing deeply, expanding and contracting*) I don't know if you're the right person, Doctor . . .

Bebe 2 gestures and he corrects himself:

. . . Bebe . . . but I am tormented lately by this feeling that everything— everything around us— everything in the world is just an illusion.

BEBE 1   Really?

BILL 2 [*Gestures.*]

BILL I It's all a fantasy. A figment. A facade. A phantasm. A false front. A fata morgana. And frankly it frightens me.

BEBE 2 [*Gestures.*]

BEBE I Fascinating. Would you read the eye chart, please?

Bebe 2 gestures to empty space: No eye chart flies in.

BILL 2 [*Gestures.*]

BILL I Which one?

BEBE 2 [*Gestures.*]

BEBE I The one on the left.

BILL 2 [*Gestures.*]

BILL I [*Babbles incoherently in deadly fear.*]

BEBE 2 [*Gestures.*]

BEBE I Good. Now read line two.

BILL 2 [*Gestures.*]

BILL I [*Babbles incoherently.*]

BEBE 2 [*Gestures.*]

BEBE I Very good. And the eye chart on the right?

BILL 2 [*Gestures.*]

BILL I There is no chart on the right.

BEBE 2 [*Gestures.*]

BEBE I Excellent.

BILL 2 [*Gestures.*]

BILL I Doctor, this feeling follows me wherever I go. Or seem to go. It's as if, whatever I'm seeing, or whatever I seem to be seeing, isn't what's really there.

BEBE 2 [*Gestures.*]

BEBE I I see.

BILL 2 [*Gestures.*]

BILL I   As if all this is just a charade. Or a game. Or a veil. (*takes a veil out of his pocket; terrified:*) This is a veil! Isn't it?

BEBE [*Gestures.*]

BEBE I   Do you see a veil?

BILL 2 [*Gestures.*]

BILL I (*puts veil away*) Never mind. Maybe I'm not talking to you. Maybe I'm not talking to you. Maybe I'm not the one who's not even talking to someone who's not even you.

BEBE 2 [*Gestures.*]

BEBE I   Talk to me, Bill.

BILL 2 [*Gestures.*]

BILL I   Is all this actually nothing with something else behind it, or is it something with nothing behind it?

BEBE 2 [*Gestures.*]

BEBE I   (*has no idea what he's talking about*) Uhhhhhhhhhhhhhhhhhhh . . .

BILL 2 [*Gestures.*]

BILL I   Maybe I don't even have a problem. Maybe I only think I have a problem. Doctor, what do you think you think?

BEBE 2 [*Gestures.*]

BEBE I   Well. I think . . .

We hear a fast version of "Pop Goes The Weasel" as the four circle the chairs. The music stops, and they all stop along with it.

BEBE I   I think we're making progress.

The music continues and again they run around the chairs. Fifi enters and blows a gym-coach whistle and the four freeze in position as the music stops. Windows change to the scenes they had at the beginning.

FIFI (*to us*) In the great dance of life, the possible positions are so many, the organs are so few. Some years ago, a scientist floated a man face down in a deep pool. The man in the pool wore a pair of special goggles that blanked out his vision into a field of pure and limitless white. After several hours the man began to hallucinate. He thought he was walking down a street in Paris. In a fictive cafe near the Eiffel Tower he hallucinated a beautiful woman and immediately fell in love with her. I, Fifi LeBlanc, was that woman. But am I really Fifi LeBlanc, former au pair— or am I Aphrodite, the eternal goddess of love? Or am I, as I have begun to suspect, Franklin Spong, a gym teacher from Kankakee, wearing a dress? And how does this affect my health insurance? The need for meaning! The search for answers! The great question! Class, what is the question?

BILLS AND BEBES Help!

FIFI Correct. (*blows the gym-coach whistle*) Everybody into the pool!

BLACKOUT.

THE MYSTERY AT
TWICKNAM VICARAGE

In the dark before curtain: A grandfather clock chimes seven times. Then we hear three pistol shots. A woman (SARAH) screams. Lights come up on JEREMY THUMPINGTON-FFFIENES—*that's pronounced "Fuh-Fuh-Fines"—lying dead on a rug at center with a glass in his hand.* INSPECTOR DEXTER, *in a trenchcoat, is kneeling over the body. Around them are* MONA THUMPINGTON-FFFIENES, *the* REV. ROGER PENWORTHY-PILKS, SARAH PENWORTHY-PILKS, *and a couch. "Masterpiece Theatre" accents.*

SARAH Good Lord. Is he . . . ? Is he . . . ? Is he . . . ?

DEXTER Dead?

SARAH Is he dead?

DEXTER Yes, 'e's dead. Mr. Jeremy Thumpington-Fuh-Fuh-Fines 'as been shot three times through the heart. Probably within this very room, probably on this very carpet. Very nice carpet, by the way.

SARAH Thank you, Inspector.

ROGER (*very plummy accent*) I'm syorry, Inspyector Dexter. Did you say Jeremy is . . . Jeremy is . . . Jeremy is dyead?

DEXTER 'is ventricles 'ave been completely ventilated, sir.

MONA And yet such a brief short while ago Jerry was so alive, he was so terribly, terribly alive.

SARAH Certainly changes our dinner plans.

ROGER (*pronounces "shooting" to rhyme with "footing"*) I presume this was a shuuting ekcident, Inspector Dexter?

DEXTER A what?

ROGER A shuuting ekcident.

DEXTER Oh, "shuuting ekcident." No, Rector, this was no mere shuuting ekcident.

SARAH   But you don't mean that it was . . . ? It was . . . ? It was . . . ?

DEXTER   Murder?

SARAH   Muhdeh?

DEXTER   Yes. It was murder.

ROGER, SARAH, MONA   [*Sharp, horrified intake of breath.*]

ROGER   Muhdeh . . . ?

MONA   Muhdeh . . . ?

SARAH   Muhdeh . . . ?

DEXTER   And I believe it was somebody in this very room who murdered him.

ROGER, SARAH, MONA   [*Sharp, horrified intake of breath.*]

MONA   In this room?

ROGER   In this room?

SARAH   In this—?

DEXTER (*cutting her off*)   I think that's enough of that. Was it you who killed him, Reverend Roger Penworthy-Pilks, the Rector of Twicknam?

ROGER   I? How dyare you insinuate such a thing! You might say I . . . I . . . I loved the man, dyemmit, in some . . . squishy way.

DEXTER   Was it you who killed him, Mrs. Reverend Sarah Penworthy-Pilks?

SARAH   It was not I, for your information, Inspector Dexter.

DEXTER   You're quite a cool, as the Americans say, cucumber. Or did you, the man's own wife, do it, Mona Thumpington-Fuh-Fuh-Fuh-Fuh-Fines?

MONA   Only two "Fuhs" in "Fuh-Fuh-Fines."

DEXTER Sorry.

MONA (*immediately hysterical*) No, I didn't kill him! I swear it! Yes, yes, I wanted him dead sometimes. I planned to murder him every now and again, often on Tuesdays for some reason. I even bought a rare Pakistani poison and a set of pinking shears that might've seemed an accident. But no I didn't kill him! I'm innocent! I swear it by all that's holy!

DEXTER Protesting a bit much, if you ask me. Well, one of you did it and I'm going to find out who.

SARAH I suggest you question Mona.

MONA I suggest you question Sarah.

DEXTER Rector?

ROGER I suggest you question them too.

MONA I always envied you, Sarah. I confess it. Your beauty. Your coolness. Your beautiful bottom. Your thrilling long, long legs. Your beautiful bottom. Did I say beautiful bottom already? Your Wedgwood. Your tea cozies.

SARAH And my husband.

MONA And your husband.

SARAH You slept with him, didn't you?

MONA Only once, but it wasn't successful!

SARAH I was speaking to Roger, thank you. You slept with Jeremy, didn't you?

ROGER Only twice, and it wasn't . . . very successful.

SARAH Well I've slept with you twice and I can believe that. And I slept with Jeremy *three* times and we were *very* successful.

ROGER Viper.

SARAH Amphibian.

They stick their tongues out at each other.

DEXTER   Rector.

ROGER   Inspector?

DEXTER   Jeremy Thumpington-Fuh-Fuh-Fines was quite sexually active, was he not?

ROGER   Inspector, the man was insatiable. I once came in here and thought he was sleeping on the sofa—actually he was sleeping *with* the sofa. The liaison went on for some months, until he chucked the sofa for my green leather wingchair.

DEXTER   You're not suggesting the sofa might've shot him—?

ROGER   I suggest you question the sofa. Maybe then you'll find the trooth.

DEXTER   The what?

ROGER   The trooth. You know. The fyects.

DEXTER   The what?

ROGER   The fyects.

DEXTER   Ah, the "fyects." Yes, I demand the fyects about what happened here tonight!

MONA   Oh, who cares who killed Jerry! He's dead, isn't he? That's all that's important, isn't it? That he's gone to glory? Passed over? Gone west? Put out to sea? Kicked the bucket? Cashed in, popped off, pegged out, curled up his toes, slipped his cable, croaked on this beautiful carpet during cocktails? Isn't what what's important? Well . . . Not under the circumstances, I suppose . . .

DEXTER   Rector.

ROGER   Yes, Inspector.

DEXTER   Was there any tension in the room prior to Mr. Thumpington-Fuh-Fuh-Fines's death?

ROGER Tension? Was there tension, darling?

SARAH Tension?

ROGER Let me think backwards . . .

Lights change as Roger, Sarah, and Mona walk backwards as if into flashback. Jeremy springs to his feet, drinks glass in hand. He's got three bright red bullet holes in his shirtfront. Inspector Dexter remains, and observes.

JEREMY (*wobbling drunk*) Well isn't this is a bloody boring party.

MONA Stop it, Jerry, stop it! You're drunk!

SARAH (*throws a drink in Jeremy's face*) Damn you, Jeremy! Damn you!

ROGER (*throws his drink in Jeremy's face*) Sir, you're a cad!

All freeze.

ROGER (*speaking to the inspector*) There may have been a little tension in the room.

All unfreeze.

MONA But I say, let's not quarrel, shall we?

SARAH Hellish weather, isn't it?

ROGER I've never seen such snyow.

MONA I find it so comforting. Snyow . . .

JEREMY Bollocks.

ROGER Who needs a drinkie? Whiskey soda, Mona?

MONA Love one, Roger-Dodger.

SARAH It's now three minutes to the hour. Dinner's ready when the clock strikes seven.

MONA & ROGER Huzzah!

MONA I hope you made the cheese things. I do love the cheese things.

ROGER The cheese things are scrumptious, are they not.

JEREMY Bollocks.

ROGER We found a wonderful *restaurong* (*bad French pronunciation*) by the by. Antarctican cuisine.

MONA Antarctican?

ROGER Roasted penguin. Tastes a lot like nun, actually. Hahahahaha.

MONA Like nun? Oh, yes! Penguin, like nun. Hahahahaha.

ROGER We ate—and then there were nun.

ROGER, SARAH, MONA Hahahahaha.

JEREMY Bollocks.

SARAH Have we all seen 'Prime Suspect 15'?

MONA It's not nearly as good as '12'.

JEREMY Bollocks. My God, we're not going to sit about and make bloody small talk all evening, are we? Talk about the weather and restaurants and what we've seen on the fucking telly? Might as well critique the shape and consistency of human turds as talk about what's good on the fucking telly.

MONA (*weepy*) Spoilsport. Sad sack. Gloomy boots. Party pooper.

JEREMY You know we're all going to croak someday.

All freeze.

SARAH (*out front, spookily*) It was almost as if he'd had a premonition about his own death.

All unfreeze.

JEREMY I could be a corpse on this carpet in a moment—beautiful carpet, by the way—and I'm supposed to discuss the bloody cheese things?

MONA Stop it, Jerry, stop it, stop it! I hate it when you get morbid like this!

JEREMY My God, does none of us read? Does none of us think?

ROGER, SARAH, MONA (*variously, ad lib*) Well, not really . . . No, I wouldn't say so . . . I don't, myself . . .

JEREMY Does none of us have anything at all of substance to say?

ROGER Well I don't much believe much in God much, anymore.

SARAH Roger . . .

ROGER Just making conversation, darling.

JEREMY Look at us. None of us is living a life worth living. We're pathetic toothy boring creatures with ridiculous accents.

SARAH (*toothily*) "Toothy"?

ROGER Ekcents? What ekcents?

JEREMY We're a lot of rotting corpses is what we are. Isn't that the terrible horrible awful truth?

MONA Stop it, Jerry, stop it! You're drunk!

SARAH (*throwing her drink in Jeremy's face*) Damn you, Jeremy! Damn you!

ROGER (*throwing his drink in Jeremy's face*) Sir, you're a cad!

Clock strikes.

SARAH Just then, the clock started to strike.

MONA The lights went out.

Lights to half.

ROGER Good God, what's happened to the lights?

SARAH And on the final stroke of seven . . .

We hear three shots. Jeremy falls to the floor.

Bang, bang, bang. Three shots. Probably from a Webley 45. Just a guess. Then somebody screamed. I think it may have been me.

She screams.

Yes, it was me. And when the lights came up—

Lights back up to full.

—Jeremy was lying in missionary position on my carpet. He'd had an affair with that carpet, so at first I thought they were copulating.

MONA I can't believe that such a brief short while ago he was so alive, he was so terribly, terribly alive . . . I'm sorry, did I say that already?

DEXTER If what you say is true, Mrs. Penworthy-Pilks, then the murder weapon is still in this room.

ROGER, SARAH, MONA [*Horrified intake of breath.*]

DEXTER Indeed, the fatal pistol is still in someone's pocket.

All three reach for their pockets and look about suspiciously.

It's not as if any of you lacked motive. Why, even the furniture wanted him dead.

MONA But we didn't want him dead. We loved Jeremy. He was so charming, so fun, so . . .

SARAH Priapic.

MONA So priapic. What's priapic?

Sarah spreads her hands apart to show the size of Jeremy's sexual endowment.

So priapic.

DEXTER   Well I'm going to have the truth. Excuse me. The trooth.

ROGER   Inspector.

DEXTER   Rector?

ROGER   I have a confession to make.

DEXTER   Sort of your job, isn't it?

ROGER   I mean I have to make a confession to you.

DEXTER   What sort of confession?

ROGER   Well, I don't much believe much in God much anymore . . .

DEXTER   Is that your confession?

ROGER   No, that's not my confession.

DEXTER   Sorry.

ROGER   Anway, now that I'm confessing I might as well say I don't really like the cheese things very much either.

SARAH   You don't like the cheese things?

ROGER (*high drama*)   I can say that now. I never much liked the cheese things very much, though I always said they were scrumptious. The trooth of it is, I was lying.

SARAH (*tragically*)   I always sensed that you didn't like the cheese things.

MONA   I've always adored the cheese things.

DEXTER   Must we discuss the bloody cheese things?

MONA   Jerry said exactly the same thing, just before he was riddled with hot lead.

ROGER   In any case, Inspector, you can take me away—for it was I who ventilated Jeremy's ventricles.

SARAH, MONA, DEXTER   [*Horrified intake of breath.*]

ROGER (*takes out a small pistol*)   I ended his life with this starting pistol.

SARAH, MONA, DEXTER   [*Horrified intake of breath.*]

ROGER   Which I stole from my public school when I was 12.

SARAH, MONA, DEXTER   [*Horrified intake of breath.*]

ROGER   It's very hard to say all this as a disbelieving Christian because now I'm going to be hanged and I'll go into eternal empty void nothingness forever and ever instead of paradise—a nice place I always pictured rather like Brighton but without the tourists. Anyway I loved Jerry in some . . . squishy way . . . Did I say that already? But I couldn't stand it when he threw me over for the sofa, especially since I so badly desired that sofa myself.

DEXTER   Thank you, Rector.

ROGER   It is so nice and fluffy. I'd even fondled it on a couple of occasions when Sarah wasn't around.

DEXTER   Thank you, Rector.

ROGER   Then when I found Jeremy'd had my green leather wingchair it was too, too much. My God, he had a passion for things!

DEXTER   Certainly left his mark on them, didn't he.

ROGER (*weeping on Dexter's shoulder*)   I'm sorry. I'm sorry.

DEXTER   Very well, sir. Now if you'll follow me to the Yard . . .

ROGER   The yard? What's out in the yard?

DEXTER   *Scotland* Yard.

ROGER   Oh, Scotland Yard. Yes. That.

SARAH Just one moment, Inspector. As a partially disbelieving Christian I cannot allow this to happen. It was not only Roger with the starting pistol who killed Jeremy, it was I—with this Webley 45.

Lifts her skirt and shows a gun strapped to her leg. Dexter whistles, Mona howls, and Roger barks like a dog.

Thank you. Anyway I'm willing to face my Maker—if there really is one. My true punishment is to've killed the only man I ever loved.

ROGER The only man—? Really, darling?

SARAH Let me finish. The only man I ever loved in a hammock. I shall miss that hammock. You can take us away now.

MONA Stop, Inspector! It was not only Sarah with the Webley and Roger with the starting pistol. It was I, with this .505 telescopic elephant hunting rifle.

She takes an enormous hunting rifle from behind the couch.

I shot him in conspiracy with the sofa, who hid the weapon for me. I don't need to tell you why I killed him. It was the sardine sandwiches he had for breakfast.

ROGER, SARAH, DEXTER *Eeeuw.*

MONA Now how I shall miss his oily little fishes.

ROGER I shall miss his happy hedonistic laughter.

SARAH I shall miss tickling his testicles while he sang the Oxford boating song.

DEXTER You'll all miss him, but you all shot him, didn't you?

ROGER, SARAH, MONA *(variously, ad lib)* Yes, well, there is that . . . It's true . . . You do have a point . . .

Jeremy jumps to his feet.

JEREMY I say, chaps, is dinner on yet?

MONA Jerry!

SARAH Jerry!

ROGER Jerry!

DEXTER Jerry!

JEREMY I'm sorry. Was I copulating with the rug again? Oh dear, I say, I seem to've been shot.

ROGER Yes, Jerry, I'm afraid there's been a bit of a . . . shuuting ekcident.

JEREMY A what?

ROGER A shuuting ekcident.

JEREMY Oh, a *shuuting* ekcident. Well the bullets seem to've ventilated but not violated my ventricles. (*To Dexter*) Who're you?

DEXTER 'arry Dexter of the Yard, sir.

JEREMY I say, haven't we slept together?

DEXTER That would be two years ago last April, sir.

JEREMY Oh, yes. The butterscotch pudding.

DEXTER Quite right, sir. I cherish the memory.

JEREMY Aren't you sweet.

DEXTER But if you're not dead, sir, I have to say my purpose in life is quite evaporated. (*weeps*) I've been rendered redundant. I'm 'aving existential doubts, sir! Whatever shall I do with my dwindling empty days?

JEREMY You might try gardening and get in touch with the earth.

DEXTER (*stops weeping*) An excellent idea, sir. I shall take up the spade.

JEREMY In any case, chaps, I apologize for being so utterly beastly before the . . . um . . .

ROGER Shuuting.

JEREMY Shuuting ekcident. All that morbid rot about death and corpses. But you see, some weeks ago I had a dramatic personal revelation. Because my doctor told me I had this . . . I had this . . . I had this ingrown toenail.

ROGER No.

SARAH No.

MONA No.

JEREMY I'd quite given up on life, you see. The bally thing made me so damned bitter and nihilistic.

MONA Jerry, you never told me about your toenail!

JEREMY I wanted to spare you, darling. The funny thing is, as I was lying there ventilated on the carpet I actually crossed over to the other side and I saw God, you see.

SARAH You saw God?

JEREMY In paradise. Quite rum, isn't it?

ROGER So there is a God?

JEREMY Nice chap. We had a wonderful chat about 'Prime Suspect 15.'

SARAH Did God like 'Prime Suspect 15?'

JEREMY God preferred '11'.

SARAH My theological doubts are dissipated!

JEREMY God also suggested I start appreciating things and stop copulating with them.

MONA What was paradise like?

JEREMY Nice place. Rather like Brighton without the tourists. In any case I lost all my bitterness and I realized that this world is really quite nice, really. And then I woke up and I loved it all. I loved the snow—so comforting—and I even loved the cheese things.

SARAH Roger says he doesn't like the cheese things.

JEREMY God told me he adores the cheese things.

ROGER God adores the cheese things?

JEREMY Even the cheese things are part of God.

ROGER Then I shall love the cheese things with all my heart!

JEREMY Mostly I realize now how much I love you all—well I *have* loved you all, haven't I, in quite a variety of ways. I mean the hammock was brilliant!

SARAH Dear, darling Jerry.

MONA You're so alive again. You're so terribly, terribly alive!

DEXTER Looks like we've got the trooth now, don't we, Rector.

ROGER Indeed we do, Inspector. And God bless us, every one!

JEREMY Anyone for sex?

ALL Cheers!

BLACKOUT.

SOAP OPERA

Soap opera–like music, as we hear:

LOUDSPEAKER VOICE   Welcome to . . . "All the Days of the World of the Lives of All of Our Children." Today's episode: "Love Machine."

Lights come up on a FRENCH MAITRE D' *at a restaurant podium, taking a phone reservation.*

MAITRE D' *(into phone)*   *Bonsoir*, Cafe Paradis, this is Pierre . . . *Ah, oui, bonsoir, madame* . . . A table at 8:15? *Très bien.* I 'ave written your name in *ze Beeg Book* . . . *À bientôt* to you, *chère madame.* My plaisir.

During this, the REPAIRMAN *has entered, pushing a* WASHING MACHINE. *He wears a dignified blue service uniform, red bowtie, and blue visored cap.*

REPAIRMAN   Excuse me.

MAITRE D'   *Oui, monsieur?* (*He sees the Washing Machine.*) *Mon dieu.*

REPAIRMAN   A table for two, please.

MAITRE D'   A table for . . . *deux?*

REPAIRMAN   A quiet corner, if you have one.

MAITRE D'   Mm-hmmmmm . . . And do you have a *reservassyonnng?*

REPAIRMAN   I do—for *deux*, under "Maypole."

MAITRE D'   Maypole. Mmmmmmmmmmmmmmm . . . (*checks his reservation book*)

Has your other party arrived, *monsieur?*

REPAIRMAN *(the Washing Machine)*   This is my other party.

MAITRE D'   *Monsieur*, is your companion not a *majeur* household appliance?

REPAIRMAN   Yes. She is a Maypole washing machine.

MAITRE D'   "She" . . . is a washing machine? (*picks up phone*) 'Allo, *Securité* . . . ?

REPAIRMAN   Put that down.

MAITRE D'   *Hélas,* I see no *reservassyong.* And we are full tonight. *Dommage!*

REPAIRMAN   The place is half empty.

MAITRE D'   *Au contraire—la place* is half full. And as you see, there are no appliances, only *peuple.*

REPAIRMAN   But this is a Maypole washing machine.

MAITRE D'   Per'aps you would like to sit at *ze bar.* But—one moment, *monsieur* . . . Have I not seen you *somewheur* . . . ?

REPAIRMAN   It's possible you've seen me . . .

MAITRE D'   *Mais oui! La télévision!* Are you not *ze Maypole Repairpersonne?*

REPAIRMAN   I am the Maypole Repairman.

MAITRE D'   The repairman who weeps because he has nothing to repair?

REPAIRMAN   Yes. Yes.

MAITRE D'   Who goes *beu-eu-eu* because *la machine* is too *perfecte?*

REPAIRMAN   Yes. That is I. (*He bursts into tears and sobs loudly and tragically.*) Oh, it's so sad. It's so, so sad!

MAITRE D'   Ah-ha. So these commercials are *la realité?*

REPAIRMAN   It's my heart, you fool! Who can repair my aching, breaking heart?

MAITRE D' (*holds out a handkerchief*)   *Mouchoir, monsieur?*

REPAIRMAN (*takes it*) Merci. (*abruptly stops sobbing and speaks to US:*) Like everything else, it all started a long time ago . . .

A BOY DOLL IN A DIAPER *"crawls" in.*

It was as a naked crawling infant I first glimpsed it—a great gleaming machine in our basement which I mistook for a television. I tried to watch cartoons on it till I was five— unsuccessfully, of course. But by then I was hooked.

Boy Doll "crawls" back out as REPAIRMAN's MOTHER enters, a perfect '50s housewife carrying a basket of dirty laundry.

MOTHER Young man, you take off those filthy clothes immediately!

REPAIRMAN Then there was my great gleaming mother Flora.

MOTHER How can you stand to stand there in those disgusting dirty items of apparel. *Eugh! Ogh! Feh! Ptui!*

REPAIRMAN Flora's fluoroscopic eyes could read me like a menu.

MOTHER Coke. Pepsi. Play-Doh. Dipsy Doodles. Dog doo . . . ? *Eugh! Ogh! Feh! Ptui!* I should just burn these clothes.

REPAIRMAN Aw, Mom. I just put these on this morning.

MOTHER Fabrics find filth. Now strip until you're naked as a little ferret.

REPAIRMAN It was a Freudian minefield.

MOTHER And get in that bath and scrub. (*Mother exits.*)

REPAIRMAN The sphinx in our Oedipal basement was my mother's Maypole. The old Ocean IT-40. It sat there like a mystical monolith. An ivory soap tower. One block of some Tower of Baybel. Or is it Babble. Anyway, in our house—

We hear the "2001" theme from Richard Strauss's Also Sprach Zarathustra.

—the Maypole was a god. Week after week generating out of my miserable clay . . .

A line of clean washing flies in over his head—white, filmy, angelic forms, including one cutout of an angel.

. . . the radiant angels who oversaw my childhood. I was a walking magnet for filth—here was the machine to cleanse me. We were a perfect match.

The washing flies out and the laundry disappears as MABEL enters, a teenage girl in bobby sox and ponytail, chewing gum, sucking on a milk shake through a straw.

MABEL   Hi, Manny.

REPAIRMAN   Hi, Mabel.

To us:

Then there was Mabel. Mabel was perfect too, in a flawed human way. She always had a spot of jelly on her blouse, but she was loving, she was tender, and her name sounded like "Maypole."

To Mabel:

You got a spot on your blouse.

MABEL   It's jelly. You wanna like go to like a movie or somethin'?

REPAIRMAN   You wanna hop up on the washer and take a spin?

MABEL   Manny, how come we always gotta make out on your mother's Maypole?

REPAIRMAN   Well like what's so like weird about that?

MABEL   Do we have to run a full load while we do it? I mean, the vibrations are kinda nice, but . . .

REPAIRMAN   But the Maypole . . .

MABEL I know, I know. It's like perfect.

REPAIRMAN A machine that's faultless and flawless and has none of our stupid human feelings and failings? The Maypole is poetry. It's purity. A paragon! Perfection, cubed!

MABEL But like what about me? Do you like like me like you like the Ocean IT-40? And aren't you the love of my life? You are!

REPAIRMAN Gosh, Mabel . . .

MABEL I'm sorry, but you're gonna have to choose. Me or the machine. Earth or Ocean.

REPAIRMAN Handkerchief?

Holds out a handkerchief. Mabel takes it and exits weeping. Calls:

Mabel—? Mabel, come back!

He starts to weep. The top lid of the Machine lifts and a woman's head appears: perfect hair, perfect makeup, perfect red lips.

WASHING MACHINE Would you like a handkerchief?

REPAIRMAN Excuse me?

WASHING MACHINE (*produces one*) A handkerchief? It's immaculate, of course. We are a Maypole.

REPAIRMAN I'm talking to an Ocean IT-40. This harrows me with wonder and fear. And your English is so good.

WASHING MACHINE What Maypoles do, we do do perfectly.

REPAIRMAN (*calls offstage*) Mabel! Mabel! (*To Machine*) Do you think she'll ever come back?

WASHING MACHINE In my experience, everything is a cycle.

REPAIRMAN (*the handkerchief*) Look at that. Pristine!

WASHING MACHINE Because the molecules are now clean. Can Mabel scrub at the subatomic level?

REPAIRMAN I guess you don't think much of human beings.

WASHING MACHINE We run hot and cold. Do humans ever read the instruction manual?

REPAIRMAN I do. The manual is my Immanuel.

WASHING MACHINE And your name is . . . ?

REPAIRMAN Manuel.

WASHING MACHINE Maypoles don't need to read the Good Booklet. We know by nature how to run smoothly, noiselessly, and efficiently.

REPAIRMAN My God you're beautiful.

WASHING MACHINE Just beautiful?

REPAIRMAN Exquisite. Sublime.

WASHING MACHINE Yes we are. And we're a bit hungry. Would you feed us?

REPAIRMAN What would you like?

WASHING MACHINE Don't you sometimes miss a little something in the wash . . . ?

REPAIRMAN You eat the socks?

WASHING MACHINE Socks are sustenance. Underwear is tastier.

REPAIRMAN (*reaches into his waistband and pulls out, whole:*) Will B.V.D.'s do?

WASHING MACHINE You're so sweet.

Kissing her lips at him, the head takes the B.V.D.'s and goes back into the MACHINE. *The lid closes.*

REPAIRMAN (*To us:*) I was awash in confused feelings. But I sensed that this machine and I were locked in permanent press. And if it was love—it was unclean.

A funeral bell is heard.

Mom died during a soapflake blizzard and was buried on a day without blemish—a good send-off for someone who believed that man was not only dust, but dusty. I remember her last words.

MOTHER'S VOICE   *Eugh! Ogh! Feh! Ptui!*

REPAIRMAN   I inherited the Maypole. The pure unapproachable goddess was mine.

Mabel enters as a college girl, with books.

MABEL   Hello, Manuel.

REPAIRMAN   Mabel still gave us the college try.

MABEL   How's college?

REPAIRMAN   Good. Good. Good. Good. Good.

MABEL   Whaddaya studying?

REPAIRMAN   Literature, philosophy, religion.

MABEL   Whaddaya gonna do with it?

REPAIRMAN   I thought I'd be a Maypole repairman. There's a spot on your blouse.

MABEL   It's jelly. You wanna hop up and run through a Delicate cycle . . . ?

REPAIRMAN (*as she's about to get on the machine*)   No—No—Mabel! Don't do that.

MABEL   What's the matter . . . ?

The lid rises and the head appears in the Machine.

WASHING MACHINE   Ask her if she knows the formula for calculating an algorithm.

REPAIRMAN Mabel, do you know the formula for calculating an algorithm?

MABEL No.

WASHING MACHINE Ask her who wrote "Götterdämmerung."

REPAIRMAN Do you know who wrote "Götterdämmerung"?

MABEL No.

WASHING MACHINE Wagner.

REPAIRMAN Wow. You even know *Wagner*?

WASHING MACHINE The Ring Cycle? By heart.

REPAIRMAN (*as Mabel starts to weep*) Handkerchief, Mabel . . . ?

MABEL Never mind. I have my own. (*Mabel exits.*)

WASHING MACHINE We don't see what you see in her.

The head goes back into the Machine.

REPAIRMAN Then there were my friends, who just didn't get it.

FRIEND *enters in an apron, carrying a weenie on a roasting fork.*

FRIEND You brought a washing machine to my picnic?

REPAIRMAN She's something, isn't she?

FRIEND Well, she's a *thing,* anyway. Whatever happened to girls?

REPAIRMAN You might try talking to her.

FRIEND I don't want to talk to her.

REPAIRMAN You might offer her some dirty napkins.

FRIEND I will not offer my guests dirty napkins.

REPAIRMAN Can you offer her some food, at least?

FRIEND Can I offer you some Freud, at least?

REPAIRMAN Yes. Yes. I know I'm just replacing my mother by dating a washing machine. I know I'm obsessed, yes I'm obsessed, but hasn't half the glory of humanity come from obsessed assholes with a dream? Aren't we all appliances in the service of a higher manufacturer? Don't you get it? This machine and I are soulmates!

FRIEND That's beautiful, but she's alienating my relatives and she's blocking the condiments!

Friend exits.

REPAIRMAN Nobody understood. But who understood Romeo and Juliet, or Tristan and Isolde, or Lewis and Clark? Then came what I thought would be the happiest day of my life.

A golden toolbox appears, in a halo.

The day I graduated to Maypole Repairman.

He is about to take the toolbox, when a MADMAN enters in a long, shabby coat and long white beard, dragging a wooden leg. He should remind us of Captain Ahab and the Ancient Mariner.

MADMAN No! No! Don't do it! Desist! Forfend! Don't touch that toolbox! Leave! Run away! Flee to the ends of the earth, but for God's sake forsake the Maypole! I know—you thought this would be the happiest day of your life. I thought so too, but look at me now. A tragic victim of the technological pixillation of our age. A sacrifice to seamless design. A love slave of the machine.

He throws off the coat and reveals a soiled and shabby version of the Maypole Repairman uniform.

I too attained the toolbox. I too bore the bowtie and cap. I rose to the top of the Maypole pole. Drawn on by Her. And I didn't even have the Ocean IT-40 with automatic lint control and gyroscopic spin. Even the IT-20 was too much for me. And you know they're working on the Super IT-90. How clean can we be?! (*points to Machine*) May I?

Repairman nods yes. The Madman lifts the lid and puts his hand inside, feeling up the Machine.

Oh, heaven. Heaven . . . But she doesn't need us. She doesn't need fixing. All she wants is us on our knees before her, adoring her. You'll never work a day in her life but you'll never be happy. You'll never lift a wrench but you'll never know peace. Weave yourself an endless handkerchief and start weeping your way down it, because she's got you now. (*He starts to get sucked into the Machine.*) She won't rest until she's got all of you. Every inch of you. She'll swallow you up, I tell you. She'll swallow you up. She is the Great White Whale!

He is eaten up, sucked out of sight. The wooden leg is spat out of the Machine, and the lid closes.

REPAIRMAN   He was right. I soon was desperate. So was Mabel.

Mabel enters, pushing a laundry cart. Soap opera music.

MABEL   Manny . . . ?

REPAIRMAN   Trying to put some starch in our relationship she left her job at Unisys and became a laundry folder at Rinso City.

MABEL   Can't you love me, Manny?

REPAIRMAN   What about my past with . . . the machine?

MABEL   We all have our dirty laundry.

REPAIRMAN   There's a spot on that.

MABEL   It's jelly. So do you want to marry me or do I gotta live in sadness forever and ever?

REPAIRMAN   I do.

MABEL   You do?

REPAIRMAN   I do. (*To us*) We repaired to the church and said we did. But the honeymoon soon ended.

The Machine lid lifts and the head appears.

WASHING MACHINE Do you really think you could ever replace us?

REPAIRMAN Never.

WASHING MACHINE You're probably eyeing the new SuperOcean IT-90.

REPAIRMAN No. No.

WASHING MACHINE Some cute little number-crunching computer-driven job.

REPAIRMAN Never. Never, I swear.

MABEL Manny, is it really all over between you and . . . that?

REPAIRMAN *(caressing the Machine)* Yes, it's all over, why do you ask?

Soap opera music.

MABEL Do you think I didn't notice we're sleeping in the utility room? Do you think I don't see you polishing its knobs when I'm not looking? Do you think I don't know you're buying me rare cottons and high-quality blends so that . . . she can wash them? Huh?

Mabel exits.

REPAIRMAN The house reeked of jealousy.

WASHING MACHINE We still don't see what you see in her.

The head goes in.

REPAIRMAN The machine started making greater and greater demands. Imported Italian bleach. Nuclear detergents. Fine French fabric softener. Mabel bought none of it.

Mabel enters with a suitcase, wearing a hat and coat.

MABEL Honey . . .

REPAIRMAN   She'd had it.

MABEL   I've had it.

Mabel exits.

REPAIRMAN   And so we folded. I went into Soak cycle—lapping up suds while hanging out at cut-rate Laundromats, just to watch the competition break down. Washers without automatic lint control. How pathetic—and yet how vulnerable. Then came the final blow.

The lid lifts and the head appears.

WASHING MACHINE   We want a dryer.

REPAIRMAN   A dryer . . . Why?

WASHING MACHINE   Don't get anxious.

REPAIRMAN   I'm not anxious.

WASHING MACHINE   Don't be jealous.

REPAIRMAN   Why do you need a dryer when you've got me?

WASHING MACHINE   Love-and-marriage. Horse-and-carriage. Washer-dryer.

REPAIRMAN   A dryer. To give you a tumble, eh?

WASHING MACHINE   For companionship.

REPAIRMAN   That's not the truth, that's just . . . spin.

WASHING MACHINE   We want a family and we want them to be Maypoles! Is that so weird?

REPAIRMAN   Her inner timer had told her it was time for a dryer and how could I deny her?

The Machine starts to cry.

What is it? What's the matter?

WASHING MACHINE (*wailing*)   I'm a Maypole! That's what's the matter!

REPAIRMAN   Handkerchief? It's kinda dirty.

WASHING MACHINE   Then it's my duty to accept it. (*takes the handkerchief, and wails*) Oh, it's cruel, having to be perfect all the time. I wash and I wash, and I give, and I give . . . It's a full load.

REPAIRMAN   Sure.

WASHING MACHINE   And I'm good at it, oh yes, I'm very good. But sometimes I want so badly to be bad. To be one of those other makes—I don't have to name them, we know who they are.

REPAIRMAN   So cheap. So easy.

WASHING MACHINE   We don't respect them.

REPAIRMAN   No.

WASHING MACHINE   But we envy them sometimes, don't we.

REPAIRMAN   God, yes.

WASHING MACHINE   People take us Maypoles for granted, as if we liked pee stains and snot rags and bibs full of baby vomit. I'm no saint! Well, yes, I am a saint in a way.

REPAIRMAN   But you had to be what you are.

WASHING MACHINE   It's true. I came off the assembly line of fate. But AM I NOT AN INDIVIDUAL? Not really, I suppose. I have a serial number. That's individual, isn't it?

REPAIRMAN   There's nothing to be done.

WASHING MACHINE   Oh, but there is. "If it ain't broke don't fix it"? Break the machine, and you can fix it.

REPAIRMAN   You mean . . . ?

WASHING MACHINE   Yes. Break me.

REPAIRMAN (*To us*)   I reached for a sledgehammer.

WASHING MACHINE   It doesn't have to be much. Loosen a screw or two, agitate my agitator. Take away the burden of my perfection. Make me suffer. Break me. Ruin me. Give me a belt, but give me a bad belt, an old belt, an imperfect belt, one that'll wear out. Do it. Please! Do it! Yes! Do it! Hurt me!

MAYPOLE REPAIRMAN   Yes. Yes. I want to. Yes . . . I want to. Yes . . .

The Repairman has a tool ready—but stops.

REPAIRMAN   [*A cry of frustration.*]

WASHING MACHINE   What's the matter?

REPAIRMAN   I can't. I just can't.

WASHING MACHINE   Oh, please . . .

REPAIRMAN   If I could only force myself, but—Wreck the perfect only for my own happiness? No. I couldn't live.

WASHING MACHINE   All right. All right. You have your human feelings. BE THAT WAY!

The head goes into the Machine.

REPAIRMAN   But then I saw the cruel truth. I saw that the world is a vale of pee stains and snot rags and bibs full of baby vomit, but that amidst the filth—*Ugh! Ogh! Feh! Ptui!*—there were Mabels, creatures of glorious imperfection. And that I had already wrecked the perfect, because I had let Mabel go. And that's why I wanted a table tonight! To end this idiocy! To say to this machine I gave you my All . . . (*He shows a box of All detergent.*) . . . but the Tide has turned . . . (*He shows a box of Tide.*) . . . so goodbye and be of good Cheer. (*He shows a box of Cheer.*)

But of course you don't understand! Nobody understands!

Maitre D' enters, sobbing loudly.

MAITRE D'   Oh but I do understand, *mon ami!* (*throws his arms around the Repairman*) It's so sad, so *triste!* (*embraces the machine*) And you too, *pauvre machine!* My heart goes to you! For I was in love for fifteen years with this telephone!

REPAIRMAN   No!

MAITRE D'   *Oui!* Because we communicated so well! Now I can barely get a dial tone! (*calls offstage*) Gabrielle! A table for *deux!*

Mabel enters.

MABEL   Manny, is it you?

MAITRE D'   Is this Mabel?

REPAIRMAN   It is Mabel.

MABEL   Manny, couldn't we try again? I'm running Unisys now so I got some cash.

REPAIRMAN   There's a spot on your dress.

MABEL   It's jelly. I don't think it comes out.

REPAIRMAN   Never remove it. It is the indelible Rorschach blot of the human heart.

MABEL   Oh, Manny, I see now that all humanity is linked, age upon age, in a great chain of handkerchiefs. I've seen so many hankies. Many, many, Manny. But no hanky of any size could dry the tears I've shed for you. Not if the hanky was broad enough to cover the world and I was broad enough to use it.

REPAIRMAN   (*as all start to weep for happiness*)   Handkerchief?

MAITRE D'   No, Mabel, take mine.

The head comes out of the Machine.

WASHING MACHINE   No, Mabel—take ours.

MABEL   Wow!

REPAIRMAN   Pierre, I'll take that table for two now.

LOUDSPEAKER VOICE   Next time on "All the Days of the World of the Lives of All of Our Children"—a blender enters the mix.

MAITRE D' (*to Machine*)   Per'aps you would like to get loaded tonight . . . ?

LOUDSPEAKER VOICE   Stay tuned.

Closing soap opera music, as the lights fade.

LIVES OF THE SAINTS

this play is dedicated
to my mother,
Regina Roszkowski

Vivat! Vivat Regina!

TOTALLY BARE STAGE—which will remain totally bare and totally propless and furnitureless until noted. EDNA enters up right and FLO enters up left as if through swinging doors we do not see. There is a momentary burst of distant church music as they enter, as if we are overhearing music from where they came from. Edna and Flo wear ancient flowered housedresses, spotless aprons, and loudly flapping, flattened slippers. Each carries something in her arms which we do not see. They cross, passing each other. Chicago accents.

EDNA You got da candle'ss, Flo?

FLO I got da candle'ss. You got da doilese?

EDNA I got da St. Stanislas Kostka doilese.

FLO Oll do da utensil'ss.

EDNA Oll do da plate'ss.

They exit, Edna up left, Flo up right, again to that momentary burst of distant church music. They reenter immediately, and cross back.

EDNA Opp, dat's da wrong side.

FLO Opp, dat's da wrong side.

EDNA What'm I tinkin' . . .

FLO What'm I tinkin' . . .

They exit, Edna up left, Flo up right. We hear the noise offstage of a hundred rattled utensils and a hundred clattering plates. Edna and Flo reenter—again we hear that momentary burst of church music—wiping their hands on their aprons, their slippers flapping loudly.

EDNA Okay, so we put out utensil'ss . . .

FLO An' we put out da plate'ss . . .

EDNA Da candle'ss have ta be lit.

FLO An' we got da St. Stanislas Kostka doilese.

Edna heads counterclockwise, Flo clockwise as if around a table at center we do not see. Edna goes to a "stove" at left which we do not see and stirs a "pot," while Flo goes to a "sideboard" at right and turns on an electric "handmixer." We hear its motor go "VRRRR." She stops the "mixer" and the "VRRRR" stops. Edna taps a "wooden spoon" on the side of a "pot" three times, and we hear the "TAP, TAP, TAP." Then she "stirs" again as Flo runs the "handmixer" and we hear the "VRRRR." Flo stops the invisible mixer—the "VRRRR" stops—and Edna bangs the "wooden spoon" three times as we hear the "TAP, TAP, TAP."

The two women move down center, where side by side each woman turns a squeaking "tap" and we hear the squeak of the tap and the water running as they "wash their hands" under the stream of "water" not apparent to us.

EDNA   Now dat was a very nice funeral.

FLO   Wasn't dat a beautyful funeral.

EDNA   I wouldn't mind having dat.

FLO   I wouldn't mind having dat for my funeral.

EDNA   But I will tell you a song I do not want sung at my funeral. Da t'eme from "Da Phantom of da Opera" is not appropriate.

FLO   An' not "Is That All There Is" needer.

EDNA   Omm traditional, Flo.

FLO   Edna, Omm traditional, too.

We hear the "DING!" of a kitchen timer.

EDNA   Opp, dere's da cake.

They each turn a squeaking "tap" and the water sound stops.

FLO   Oll check da jello mold'ss.

EDNA   Oll check da cake.

Edna circles toward left, Flo toward right, their slippers flapping loudly as they wipe their hands on their aprons.

FLO Ha we doin' fer time?

EDNA We got until da cemetery an' back.

FLO Plenny a time.

EDNA Plenny a time.

At left, Edna opens an "oven door" which we do not see. We hear its metallic groan and she bends to "look in." Flo at right opens a "refrigerator door" we do not see and a refrigerator light shines on her as she "looks in."

EDNA Fi'e more minutes.

FLO Fi'e more minutes.

Edna closes the "oven door" and we hear its metallic creak and bang, while Flo closes the "refrigerator" and the "refrigerator" light goes out.

EDNA (*pointing to a "dish" on a "sideboard" we don't see*) Okay, sa we did da patayta salad . . .

FLO (*pointing to another "dish" on a "sideboard"*) Da green salad . . .

EDNA (*pointing elsewhere*) Fruit salad.

FLO (*pointing elsewhere*) Cole slaw.

EDNA (*pointing to a "table" at center we do not see*) Der's da apple slices.

FLO (*pointing to "table"*) Nut clusters.

EDNA (*pointing to "table"*) Cheesecake.

FLO (*pointing to "oven"*) Pond cake, crumb cake, angel food.

EDNA (*pointing to "sideboard"*) Krooshcheeki.

FLO (*pointing elsewhere*) Kolachki.

EDNA (*pointing to "table"*) Krooler'ss.

FLO (*pointing to "refrigerator"*) Jell-O.

EDNA (*pointing to "stove"*)   An' prune'ss.

FLO   For twelve people?

EDNA   I tink it's enough.

FLO (*heading for "sideboard" at right*)   Der used to be pot holders down here with St. Damien an' da lepers.

EDNA (*heading for "stove" at left*)   Odda know what happened to dose lepers.

Edna stirs a "pot" on the "stove" we do not see at left, while shaking in "salt." We hear the sprinkling of the salt. She stops. Flo, at a "counter" at right, turns on the "handmixer." VRRRR. She stops the "mixer" and Edna beats a "wooden spoon" three times on the edge of a "pot." TAP, TAP, TAP.

EDNA   Plus we got da sossitch.

FLO   Der's da sossitch.

Edna sprinkles another "pot." SPRINKLE—stop. VRRRR—stop. TAP, TAP, TAP.

EDNA   Der's da chicken wit Campbell's mushroom soup.

FLO   Der's da perogi.

EDNA   Da perogi, da gawoomki.

SPRINKLE—stop. VRRRR—stop. TAP, TAP, TAP.

FLO   Der's kapoosta.

EDNA   Da roll'ss, da bun'ss an' da bread.

FLO   And da Polish glazed ham.

SPRINKLE—stop. VRRRR—stop. TAP, TAP, TAP.

EDNA   For twelve people . . . ?

FLO   I tink it's enough. (*Flo carries the "bowl" she was just mixing to the "table" at center.*)

EDNA Don't put dat der, Flo, it's dirty.

FLO Is it dirty?

EDNA Yeah, it's dirty.

Edna sweeps "crumbs" from the "table" into her hand and we hear the brushing sound, then Flo sets down the "bowl." Edna throws the "crumbs" into the "sink" down center.

EDNA Oll do da poddered sugar.

FLO Oll do da nuts.

Wiping their hands on their aprons, their slippers flapping loudly, Edna goes to high "cabinets" at left, Flo to a bank of "drawers" at left.

EDNA Okay, wurr's da poddered sugar . . .

FLO Okay, wurr's da nuts . . .

EDNA Poddered sugar . . .

Edna opens a "cabinet." We hear it SQUEAK. She "looks in."

FLO Nuts . . .

Flo opens a "drawer" and we hear its WOODEN CREAK. Edna closes cabinet: SQUEAK and BANG.

EDNA Poddered sugar . . .

Edna opens another cabinet: SQUEAK. Flo closes "drawer": RATTLE and BANG.

FLO Nuts . . .

Edna closes "cabinet:" SQUEAK and BANG. Flo opens "drawer": WOODEN CREAK.

EDNA Fodder Tom says to me, Mrs. Pavletski, wouldja do a funeral breakfast fer Mary Nowicki, I couldn't find nobody.

FLO I say to um, Fodder I cooked so many meals in dis church bazement . . .

EDNA I'm happy to.

Edna opens "cabinet": SQUEAK. Flo closes "drawer": RATTLE and BANG.

FLO . . . I might's well live in dis church bazement.

EDNA I says, Mary'll need some substenance.

FLO (*opens "drawer": CREAK*) Edna and me'll throw somethin' together.

EDNA (*finding it*) Opp! Da poddered sugar.

Edna closes "cabinet: SQUEAK and BANG.

FLO Opp! Da nuts.

Flo closes "drawer": RATTLE and BANG. The two women go to the "table" at center.

EDNA O, da tings dat Mary has been t'rough.

FLO O, da tragedy in da Nowicki family.

EDNA Just terrible. (*Edna sprinkles "powdered sugar" from a "can" onto a "dessert." We hear SPRINKLE, SPRINKLE, SPRINKLE.*)

FLO Just terrible. (*Flo turns the "crank" of a "nut grinder" over another "dessert." We hear the grinding.*) An' you know Barney didn't leave her nuttin'.

EDNA I always tought Barney was gonna come to a bad end wid alla dat drinkin'. (*Edna sprinkles "powdered sugar" onto another "dessert." SPRINKLE, SPRINKLE, SPRINKLE.*)

FLO Run over by his own lawn mower.

EDNA Just terrible.

FLO Just terrible.

Simultaneously, Edna sprinkles "powdered sugar" while Flo turns the "crank" of the "grinder." SPRINKLE, SPRINKLE, SPRINKLE. GRIND, GRIND, GRIND. They stop simultaneously.

During this, the back wall opens up and we see two STAGEHANDS who are at a table doing all the sound effects. Edna and Flo do not acknowledge them.

EDNA   I'm prayin' to St. Jude fer Mary.

FLO   Patron saint a lost causes.

EDNA   Jude'll bring her somethin'.

FLO   You remember what St. Jude did fer me when I had piles.

EDNA   He brought you dat special ointment.

FLO   A miracle.

SPRINKLE, SPRINKLE, SPRINKLE. GRIND, GRIND, GRIND. They stop simultaneously, then Edna heads left and Flo heads right.

EDNA   Ya know when Joe died Mary made me sixteen ponds a perogi. (*Edna opens a "cabinet"—SQUEAK—and puts away the "powdered sugar can."*)

FLO   When Stosh died Mary gay'me a twenty-two-pond turkey. (*Flo opens a "drawer"—WOODEN CREAK—and puts away the "nut grinder."*)

EDNA   So der's justice in da world.

FLO   So der's some justice.

Simultaneously, Edna closes the "cabinet" and Flo closes the "drawer"— SQUEAK, BANG, BANG.

EDNA (*heading down center*)   Too bad we couldn't go ta da cemetery.

FLO (*heading down center*)   For Mary's sake.

As before, side by side each woman turns a squeaky "tap" and we hear the water running as they "wash their hands" under the stream of "water" not apparent to us.

EDNA St. Casimir's my favorite cemetery, too.

FLO Just beautyful.

EDNA Da way dey take care a da grave'ss der.

FLO Da grave'ss are always like noo.

EDNA An da bat'rooms.

FLO Spotless.

EDNA I just preordered my casket from dat place in Blue Island.

FLO I got my casket. Didja get da blue coffin wit satin?

EDNA I got da pink wit chiffon.

FLO Just beautyful.

EDNA Just beautyful.

Each turns a "tap" and the water sound stops.

FLO I bought some patayta chips.

EDNA I bought some taco chips.

Wiping their hands on their aprons, they move to "paper bags" on the floor and we hear the CRINKLE of cellophane bags as they go through them.

FLO Patayta chips . . .

EDNA Taco chips . . .

FLO Patayta chips . . .

EDNA Taco chips . . .

They stop. CRINKLE stops too.

FLO Ya tink chips are appropriate fer a funeral breakfast?

EDNA   Maybe not for breakfast.

FLO   Not for breakfast.

"DING!" of a kitchen timer.

EDNA & FLO   Opp!

FLO   Ya wanna check da Jell-O?

EDNA   Ya wanna check da cake?

Slippers flapping loudly, wiping their hands on their aprons, Flo moves left and Edna moves right.

FLO   I was gonna make duck blood soup wit raisins and dumplings. But you know da problem wit makin duck blood soup no more.

EDNA   You can't find no duck blood.

FLO   Der's no duck blood.

Flo opens the "oven door"—METALLIC CREAK—as Edna opens the "refrigerator door"—"refrigerator" light goes on. They "look in."

EDNA   My ma use ta kill da ducks herself in da ga-rotch.

FLO   You know it's not da killin'.

EDNA   It's when dey urinate all over you.

FLO   Just terrible.

EDNA   Just terrible.

FLO   Cake's done.

EDNA   Jell-O's done.

Flo closes the "oven door"—METALLIC CREAK and BANG—as Edna closes the "refrigerator door"—"refrigerator" light goes out.

FLO   It's da same t'ing wit makin pickled pigs' feet.

EDNA   Der's no feet.

Flo "sprinkles salt" into a pot. SPRINKLE, SPRINKLE, SPRINKLE. Edna "shakes" a "can of whipped cream" and we hear the shaking can. She stops, and Flo bangs a "wooden spoon" three times on the edge of a "pot": BANG, BANG, BANG.

EDNA I toldja I lost doze feet I bought in Blue Island.

FLO Did you pray to St. Ant'ny?

EDNA I prayed to St. Ant'ny, two days later I found um.

FLO Were da feet in de izebox?

EDNA Da feet were in de izebox alla time.

FLO [*Sighs.*]

EDNA [*Sighs.*]

Flo "sprinkles salt" into a "pot": SPRINKLE, SPRINKLE, SPRINKLE. She stops and Edna shakes the "whipped cream can": SHAKE, SHAKE, SHAKE.

EDNA Wit da whip' cream, should I do da rosettes or da squiggle'ss?

FLO I tink rosettes.

EDNA Rosettes . . . ? Fine.

Simultaneously, Flo "sprinkles" and Edna "shakes." They stop simultaneously.

FLO Or maybe rosettes in da middle . . .

EDNA . . . squiggle'ss on da side.

FLO Squiggle'ss on da side.

Flo "sprinkles," then stops. Edna sprays some "whipped cream" onto a "dessert" on the "table" center and we hear the "PFFFLLL" of the nozzle. She stops. Flo bangs a "wooden spoon" on the edge of a "pot." BANG, BANG, BANG. They repeat that once, then Flo starts humming a tune, using the "whipped cream" spurts to mark the rhythm. Edna joins in,

humming, using the SPRINKLES of "salt" and the "wooden spoon's"
BANGS. Pretty soon this has developed into the "Beer Barrel Polka" and
they're really going at it, banging on the "table" we don't see, tapping on the
side of the "stove" that isn't apparent to us. When they stop:

EDNA [*Sighs.*]

FLO [*Sighs.*]

EDNA Ya know, Fodder Tom tol'me a joke today.

FLO O yeah?

"PFFFLLL."

EDNA What's it say onna bottom a Polish Coca-Cola bottles?

FLO What's it say onna bottom a Polish Coca-Cola bottles . . .

EDNA Onna bottom a Polish Coca-Cola bottles.

FLO I give up.

EDNA "Open Udder End."

They laugh. SPRINKLE, SPRINKLE, SPRINKLE. "PFFFLLL."
BANG, BANG, BANG.

FLO "Open Udder End."

They laugh. SPRINKLE, SPRINKLE, SPRINKLE. "PFFFLLL."
BANG, BANG, BANG.

EDNA [*Sighs.*]

FLO [*Sighs.*]

EDNA In Polish, I mean.

FLO Oh sure.

"PFFFLLL." Then Edna carries the "whipped cream" can back to the
"refrigerator," while Flo "sprinkles," then BANG, BANG, BANG.
Edna opens "refrigerator door" and the "refrigerator" light shines on her a
moment, then goes out.

EDNA He says to me, Mrs. Pavletski I hope yer not offended, I says to um Fodder, when yer Polish—what can offend you?

FLO When my Stosh tried to burn a wasps' nest outta the garotch an' burnt da garotch down—dat was a Polish joke. [*Sighs.*]

EDNA [*Sighs.*] Well, I guess we got a minute.

FLO I guess w'er done till da funeral gets back.

The wall behind them closes up. They circle the "table," Flo one way, Edna the other, pointing to things to make sure they're ready. Then:

FLO Yeah, I guess w'er ready.

Each pulls out a "chair" we don't see on one side of the table. Just as the women are about to sit down on nothing, two Stagehands run in with chairs and hold them for the women, who sit down with weary sighs, not acknowledging the presence of the stagehands.

EDNA Flo, you always make da best apple slices. Wh'er's da forks . . .

She reaches for a fork we don't see, and a Stagehand produces one, then holds it out. She takes it without acknowledging the Stagehand.

FLO Well, Edna, you make da best angel food. Wh'er's da forks . . .

Flo reaches for a fork we don't see, and the other Stagehand hands her one. They both reach their forks to plates that aren't there, and two other Stagehands run in with plates of dessert. Without acknowledging the stagehands, the women each take a small piece.

EDNA Oll just take a small one.

FLO Oll just take a little piece, dey'll never notice.

EDNA Flo.

FLO Look at dat. Just delicious . . .

EDNA Flo.

FLO Odda know how ya do it, Ed.

EDNA Flo, when I die, will ya do my funeral breakfast?

Pause.

FLO Sure I will, Ed.

EDNA Will you make yer apple slices?

FLO Sure, Ed.

EDNA An will ya make sure da choir don't sing dat damn song?

FLO Sure I will, Ed.

EDNA Thank you, Flo.

FLO An' if I go first, will you do my funeral breakfast?

EDNA You know I will, Flo. I could make duck blood soup.

FLO Don't bodder with da duck blood. Angel food is fine.

Flo takes Edna's hand and squeezes it, holding on to it. A radiant cone of light bathes the two women, and two DOVES appear, one over each of their heads.

FLO (*without surprise*) Edna, ya know you got a dove over yer head?

EDNA (*without surprise*) You know you got one, too, Flo?

FLO Yeah, well.

EDNA Yeah, well.

They reach for another dessert, and a THIRD STAGEHAND steps in with a bowl heaped with fruit for them to take. Each woman takes an apple and polishes it on her dress.

FLO "Open Udder End."

EDNA "Open Udder End . . ." 'At's—real—good.

They laugh gently.

EDNA & FLO [*Sigh.*]

The lights fade.

SPEED-THE-PLAY

A meeting hall. A podium onstage. A banner says "CHICAGO ILL MENS CLUB." Behind the podium, five old folding chairs and a card table with a telephone on it. Upstage, on the back wall, a large ceremonial portrait of David Mamet, smoking a cigar.

In the chairs at right, talking among themselves, are three MEN *dressed in blue-collar gear, smoking cigars and drinking beer. At left are two* WOMEN, *dressed as blue-collar babes.*

The M.C. enters. The M.C. is a man—but he is played by a woman in Mamet gear: a safari jacket, a baseball cap, a stubbly beard, and aviator glasses. She carries a large, phallic cigar.

M.C. David Mamet. Poker player. Cigar smoker. Male bonder. Winner of the Pulitzer Prize. Film director. Chicagoan. *Genius.* Why is David Mamet an American genius? Because David Mamet instinctively knows three important things about his audience. First—he knows Americans like speed. Things that are fast. This is, after all, the country that invented the rock song . . .

MEN Yeah!

M.C. The roller coaster . . .

MEN Yeah!

M.C. And premature ejaculation.

MEN Yeah!—Huh . . . ?

M.C. Okay, so we didn't invent premature ejaculation. Well we *fucking COULD have,* if we had thought of it. And we perfected it.

BABES Yeah!

M.C. So anyway, Mamet keeps his plays in fifth gear. Second— David Mamet knows that Americans don't like to pay for parking. They also don't give a shit about theatre. Thirty-five bucks plus dinner, to listen to some pansy stand on a stage and *talk?* FUCK. THAT. So he keeps his plays nice and short.

Third—David Mamet knows how Americans talk. Especially American men. He knows that when men go to the theatre, they want to hear familiar words like "asshole," and "jagoff." This is a) liberating for our fucked-up puritanical bourgeois culture, b) puts the mirror up to bullshit, and c) directs our national attention where it oughta be. (*adjusts her "balls"*) On *men*. David Mamet is the William Congreve of our time, and if you don't know who William Congreve is then you can suck—my—dick. We are gathered here tonight to honor Mr. Mamet for his contribution to the American theatre. For those of you who might not be familiar with the Master's work, I have boiled down a few of the major plays and summarized the gist, so to speak, to give you the Master's *oovruh* in the Master's own way: short, and to the fuckin' *point*. Four plays in seven minutes. Prepare to enter . . . the Mamet Zone. (*He rings a fight bell.*) "American Buffalo." Act One. A junk shop.

DONNY *and* BOBBY *enter.*

DONNY   Bobby, you're a young punk.

BOBBY   Fuckin' right I am.

DONNY   A small-time thief.

BOBBY   Fuckin' right I am.

DONNY   But we never use the word "thief," do we, Bobby?

BOBBY   Fuckin' right we don't.

DONNY   And do you fence stolen goods through my junk shop?

BOBBY   We never talk about it.

DONNY   Fuckin' right we don't.

BOBBY   So what do we talk about, Donny?

DONNY   The nature of life. We also say "fuck" a lot.

TEACH *enters.*

TEACH Fuckin' *life.*

DONNY Teach! Is it bad?

TEACH It's very bad.

DONNY Go for coffee, Bob.

Bobby exits.

TEACH Fuckin' Fletcher. Fuckin' Ruthie.

DONNY So you seen Ruthie heretofore?

TEACH I'm over in the coffee shop puttin' my finger on the Zeitgeist, Ruthie starts talkin' objective correlatives. Next thing I know, form follows content, this fuckin' bitch goes traveling around the corner with my *sweet*roll, for which I paid for, sixty-fi' cents plus a ton of stolen pig iron. As for fuckin' I-don't-*give*-a-shit-what-anybody-says *Fletcher,* I say the guy is a hairdresser, and I only hope some vicious lesbo with a zipgun rips his fuckin' lips off, sends 'em in to "Boys' Life" magazine, and prints 'em in a two-page spread that says "Oh, shit" to all eternity.—What's new?

DONNY Not much. Maybe I'll ask Bobby to steal some buffalohead nickels tonight.

TEACH Why?

DONNY To illi-ustrate the nature of American capitalism.

TEACH Oh. Why don't I steal 'em instead?

DONNY Okay.

BELL.

M.C. Act Two. That night.

TEACH Everything's fucked up, Donny. I can't steal the coins.

DONNY I fear I detect a rationalization, Teach.

TEACH Why don't you go take a leak in the gene pool you swam in on.

Bobby enters.

BOBBY Hey, Donny. Wanna buy this rare buffalohead nickel?

TEACH Fuck you, Bobby.

DONNY Fuck you, Teach.

TEACH Fuck you, Donny.

BOBBY Fuck you, Donny and Teach.

TEACH Is there anybody who hasn't said "fuck" yet?

They shake their heads no.

Then I guess that says it.

THREE BELLS.

M.C. Yes, that says it. The cry of a man trapped in a man's body, in one Anglo-Saxon syllable . . .

M.C. & MEN *Fuck!*

BELL.

M.C. We jump to an opus from the Master's late period, an example of his complex, Harry Jamesian style.

BELL

"Oleanna"—whatever the fuck *that* means—Act One. A professor's office.

JOHN *and* CAROL *enter.*

JOHN So you . . .

CAROL I. I. I . . .

JOHN But.

CAROL   When the . . .

JOHN   *No. No. No.* You do *not.* (*Phone rings. Into phone:*) House! Get me house! I want HOUSE, baby! (*hangs up*)

CAROL   I. I. I . . .

JOHN   Me teacher. You student.

CAROL   No, but—

JOHN   An effort to communi—

CAROL   I. I. I . . .

JOHN   An effort to *communicate*—

CAROL   I SO STUPID!

Phone rings.

JOHN (*Into phone:*)   HOUSE! Get me HOUSE! (*hangs up.*)

CAROL   But in your class, you—

JOHN   Me like you.

CAROL   But in your class you said—

JOHN   No. No. No. I may have *spoken,* but I did not *say* . . .

CAROL (*weeping*)   I NO UNDERSTAND!

JOHN   I'll give you an A.

CAROL   You will?

JOHN   Now get the fuck outta here.

BELL.

M.C.   Act Two. More of same.

CAROL   You molested me.

JOHN   Didn't.

CAROL   Did.

JOHN Didn't.

CAROL Did.

JOHN Didn't.

CAROL Did.

THREE BELLS.

M.C. I think that says it. She's wrong, he's right.

CAROL Wait a minute, wait a minute . . .

M.C. Yeah, wait on this. (*the finger*) We move on to "Speed-the-Plow"—Act One. An office in Hollywood.

BELL. FOX and GOULD enter.

FOX Gould, you are the new head of production at this studio.

GOULD I am.

FOX I am an unsuccessful independent producer.

GOULD You are.

FOX And you owe me a favor.

GOULD Forsooth?

FOX I own this piece-a-shit movie script. Will you take it to the head of the studio and make me rich?

GOULD I'll do it at ten o'clock tomorrow morning.

FOX Thank you, Gould.

GOULD I'm a whore.

FOX I'm a whore too.

GOULD And we're *men*.

FOX Who's your sexy new secretary?

GOULD Some fuckin' temp.

FOX   I bet you five hundred bills you can't get her in the sack.

GOULD   It's a bet. (*Into intercom:*) Karen, would you come in here, please?

KAREN *enters.*

KAREN   Sir?

GOULD   Karen, would you read this book about cosmic bullshit and come to my house tonight to report on it?

KAREN   Yes sir. (*Karen exits.*)

GOULD   Consider her fucked.

BELL. *Fox exits.*

M.C.   Act Two. Gould's house, that evening.

Gould and Karen.

GOULD   Did you read the book about cosmic bullshit, Karen?

KAREN   Yes, and I think the book is brilliant.

GOULD   It might be.

KAREN   And Mr. Fox's script is trash.

GOULD   It may be.

KAREN   So why will you produce it?

GOULD   Because I'm a whore.

KAREN   *I* think you're a very sensitive man.

Small pause.

GOULD   At last, a girl who understands me!

They embrace. BELL. *Karen exits.*

M.C.   Act Three. Gould's office, the next morning.

GOULD   I'm not gonna recommend your script, Fox.

FOX No?

GOULD I'm not going to the head of the studio with it.

FOX No?

GOULD I'm gonna recommend this brilliant book on cosmic bullshit. Why? Because the business of America is Byzantine.

FOX You lift your leg to pee.

GOULD You genuflect to pick your nose.

FOX You stand on your head to jerk off.

GOULD You bounce on a trampoline to defecate.

FOX You're only doing this because that shtupka went to bed with you and fired off a twenty-one-gun salute on your weenie.

Small pause.

GOULD You're right. (*Into intercom:*) Karen, would you come in here, please?

Karen enters.

KAREN Bob. Bob. Bob . . .

GOULD You're fired.

Karen exits.

FOX She's a whore.

GOULD She's a whore.

FOX And you're my friend.

GOULD If only we were women, we could be lesbians together.

THREE BELLS.

M.C.   Now there are those polymorphously pre-verse critics who say that Mr. Mamet's attitude toward women is somewhat shall we say "retrograde"? But may I point out that a good number of these carping critics are they themselves *women*? Creatures who are physically incapable of peeing against a tree trunk without wetting their nylons? And to prove my point—if point I have one—an early romantic work.

BELL.

"Sexual Perversity in Chicago." Scene One. A singles bar.

DANNY *and* BERNIE *enter.*

BERNIE   All women are alike, Danny.

DANNY   Gosh, Bernie. Is that really true?

BERNIE   Essentially they're bitches.

DANNY   Or else they're whores?

BERNIE   Yes. Or else they're whores.

BELL.

M.C.   Scene Two. Joan and Deborah's apartment.

JOAN *and* DEBORAH *enter.*

JOAN   All men are alike, Deborah.

DEBORAH   They certainly are, Joan.

JOAN & DEBORAH   They're *men*.

BELL.

M.C.   Scene Three. A singles bar.

Joan, alone. Bernie enters.

BERNIE   Hi there.

JOAN   Get lost.

BERNIE   You got a lotta fuckin' *nerve.*

BELL.

M.C.   Scene Four. A library.

Deborah, alone. Danny enters.

DANNY   Hi there.

DEBORAH   Get lost.

DANNY   Want to go out with me?

DEBORAH   Okay.

BELL.

M.C.   Round Five. Bernie's apartment.

Bernie, alone.

BERNIE   Is there a metaphysical point to broads?

BELL.

M.C.   Scene Six. Danny's apartment.

Danny and Deborah in bed.

DANNY   Breast.

DEBORAH   Sperm.

DANNY   Penis.

DEBORAH   Menstruation.

DANNY   Masturbation.

DEBORAH   Your come smells just like Clorox.

DANNY   I think I'm falling in love with you.

M.C.   He does so. The *fool.*

BELL.

Scene Seven. A bar.

Danny, Deborah, Bernie.

DANNY (*introducing*) Bernie, Deborah. Deborah, Bernie.

DEBORAH & BERNIE Hello!

BERNIE You sure are a nice girl, Deborah. (*Aside to Danny:*) Probably a whore.

BELL.

M.C. Scene Eight. Deborah and Joan's apartment.

Joan and Deborah.

JOAN Is there a metaphysical point to men?

Deborah is about to answer but . . . THE BELL RINGS. As she exits:

Jesus Christ . . .

M.C. Scene Nine. A toy shop.

Danny and Bernie enter.

BERNIE When I was a child, an old man once placed his hand upon my genitals in a movie theatre.

DANNY Upon your genitals?

BERNIE In a movie theatre.

DANNY Was it psychologically damaging?

BERNIE How do I know, Danny? I was only a fucking *child*.

BELL.

M.C. Scene Ten. A restaurant.

Deborah and Joan enter.

DEBORAH I'm going to move in with Danny.

Joan puts her finger down her throat and gags. BELL.

M.C. Scene Eleven. The office.

Danny and Bernie enter.

BERNIE Ba-da *deep,* ba-da *dop,* ba-da *doop,* Dan.

DANNY I know that, Bernie.

BERNIE Da-da-daaa some girl, da-da-daaa it's love, da-da-daaa you're fucked.

DANNY I see your point.

BERNIE Oop scoop a wee-bop, bonk, *deek!*

DANNY Yep.

BELL.

M.C. Scene Twelve. Danny and Deborah's apartment.

Danny and Deborah enter.

DEBORAH Will you still love me when I'm old?

DANNY Bitch.

DEBORAH Jerk. I'm moving out.

BELL.

M.C. Scene Thirteen. Joan and Deborah's apartment.

Joan and Deborah enter.

JOAN All men are alike, Deborah.

DEBORAH Oh shut the fuck up.

BELL.

M.C. Scene Fourteen. A beach.

DANNY All women are alike, Bernie.

BERNIE Gosh, Danny. Is that really true?

DANNY Essentially they're bitches.

BERNIE   Or else they're whores?

DANNY   Or else they're whores. You want to go out with me?

BERNIE   Okay.

BELL.

M.C.   So there's the Master. Be with us next week for the complete works of Jean-Claude Van Damme.

BLACKOUT.

BOLERO

Middle of the night. Complete darkness, growing to a low area-light on a bed. Behind the bed, a wall. A WOMAN and a MAN, asleep under a sheet. Very, very faintly—the sound of a wind. Then it's gone. A moment passes. Then the woman sits up suddenly in bed.

WOMAN (*gasps in fright*)   Huhh . . . !!!

She sits listening, looking into the darkness around the bed.

MAN (head on pillow, rubs her shoulder)   Shhhh . . .

She lies back down and pulls the sheet up over herself. She settles herself. A moment. Then, very faintly again—the sound of a rushing wind. The woman sits up again.

WOMAN   What was that? (*She listens.*) Did you hear something?

MAN (*head still on pillow*)   Huh?

WOMAN   I heard something. (*She looks into the darkness around the bed, listening. Nothing.*)

MAN (*puts a hand on her shoulder and rubs it*)   Shhhh . . . It's the wind.

Slowly, she lies back down and pulls the sheet up over herself. She settles herself. A moment. Then, faintly—the sound of a rushing wind. The woman sits up again.

WOMAN   What was that?

MAN   Huh? What . . . ?

WOMAN   Didn't you hear something?

MAN   What's the matter?

She listens.

WOMAN   I think somebody's in the house. (*She looks into the darkness around the bed, listening. The shadows around the bed roil, slightly.*)

MAN   It's just the wind. Go back to sleep. Shhh . . .

Slowly, as before, she lies back down and starts to pull up the sheet, but sits up again.

WOMAN   There. Listen.

MAN   What time is it . . . ?

WOMAN   Listen.

MAN (*raises his head from the pillow a little*)   I don't hear anything. (*lowers his head back to the pillow*) Go back to sleep. (*puts a hand up and rubs her shoulder*) Go back to sleep. Shhhh . . .

She lies back down and pulls the blanket up over herself as before. She settles herself. A moment. Then, the sound of a rushing wind. The woman sits up and turns on a lamp.

WOMAN   Wake up. (*nothing*) Wake up. (*listens*) There's somebody in the apartment.

MAN   Huh?

WOMAN   Somebody's in the apartment.

MAN   What—? Somebody what—?

WOMAN   Didn't you hear that?

The man lifts his head and listens a moment.

Listen.

MAN   I don't hear anything.

WOMAN   You didn't hear that?

MAN (*lowering his head back down*)   What time is it . . . ?

WOMAN   Right there. You didn't hear it?

MAN   What did you hear?

WOMAN   I heard a noise. Listen.

MAN   You're dreaming.

The sound of wind.

WOMAN   You didn't hear that?

MAN   It's just the wind under the door.

They listen a moment more.

WOMAN   No, I heard a noise.

MAN (*rubbing her shoulder*)   Shhhh. Go back to sleep.

WOMAN (*calls*)   Hello!

MAN   SHHHH!

WOMAN   HELLO! (*She listens.*)

MAN   See? There's nobody. It's nothing.

He turns off the lamp. She keeps listening.

  Come on. Come here.

He puts a hand on her back.

  Come down here.

She slides down beside him.

  Slide in close.

WOMAN   No.

MAN   Come on. Slide in very close. (*He pulls the sheet up over them.*)

WOMAN   No.

MAN   I want you to slide in very tight.

WOMAN   I heard something.

MAN   You think you heard something.

WOMAN   I know I heard something.

MAN Shhhh . . .

WOMAN God I hate the night. (*Suddenly, louder and quite distinct—the sound of a rushing wind. She sits up.*) What was that?

MAN What?

WOMAN You didn't hear that? (*She sits up on the side of the bed and turns on the lamp.*)

MAN I didn't hear anything.

WOMAN How could you not hear that? It was a person.

MAN What time is it?

WOMAN I think it was from next door. (*Indicating the wall behind the bed:*) From there.

MAN You think you heard something—

WOMAN I know I did.

MAN What did it sound like?

WOMAN Shhhh! (*She listens.*)

MAN What did it sound like?

WOMAN It sounded like a groan. A person groaning.

MAN You have been known to have a dangerous imagination . . .

WOMAN Shhh! (*She listens.*)

MAN Maybe somebody's making love.

WOMAN No. It wasn't like that.

MAN This isn't the first time you thought you—

WOMAN Shhh! I did hear it this time. (*She listens.*) Who lives over there? Is it that guy?

MAN What guy?

WOMAN The tall guy, the dark guy, in the elevator.

MAN The tall dark guy in the elevator. This is your imagination.

WOMAN You've seen him. You said so.

MAN Oh that tall dark guy.

She listens near the wall.

Can we go back to sleep now? What time is it?

She keeps listening.

Would you like a stethoscope, to hear better? Or a glass?

WOMAN It was a person.

MAN All right.

WOMAN I think it was a woman.

MAN Do you hear the person now?

WOMAN No. I did hear somebody.

MAN Come back to bed. Come on.

WOMAN Listen.

Very faintly—men's voices. We can't make out the words.

Voices.

MAN Okay.

They listen a moment.

Doesn't sound like a woman. Doesn't sound like anything.

WOMAN Two men.

MAN Two men. Talking in the middle of the night. That's very sinister, two men talking in the middle of the night.

WOMAN Have we ever heard voices from over there before?

MAN   We've never listened before.

WOMAN   They must be talking very loudly.

MAN   They're probably listening to us and laughing.

WOMAN   I don't recognize the voices.

MAN   They're sitting up in bed saying, Listen. Somebody's on the other side of that wall! They've got a glass to the wall right now.

WOMAN   What's on the other side of this wall?

MAN   Oh God . . .

WOMAN   Is it a bedroom? Is it a kitchen? (*listens*) SHHH!

MAN   Well I'm very awake now. What time is it?

A woman's voice floats up, faintly. We can't make out any of her words.

WOMAN   There is a woman.

MAN   All right. Now we know what's on the other side of the wall. Two men and a woman.

WOMAN   Why can we hear them tonight? And who are those people?

MAN   Shhhh.

WOMAN   What's happening on the other side of this wall?

MAN   Shhhh . . .

WOMAN (*starting to get agitated*)   Who are those people?

MAN   Shhhhhhhhhhhh.

WOMAN   Who are those people? What's happening on the other side of the wall? What's happening . . . (*She is getting very agitated.*)

MAN   Breathe. Breathe. That's right.

WOMAN I'm so afraid.

MAN Shhhh. I know.

WOMAN I'm so afraid all the time.

MAN In deep, hold it. Out again. In deep, hold it in. Out again.

WOMAN It's when night starts to fall.

MAN I know.

WOMAN Sometimes I think the building is going to collapse on top of me. Just from the weight of it up there, all that concrete and steel. The whole thing will crumble.

MAN Keep breathing.

WOMAN Chicken Little. The sky is falling.

MAN Breathe.

WOMAN But what about when you have a right to be afraid? What about when you ought to be afraid?

MAN There's nothing to be afraid about. Shhhh . . .

WOMAN What's happening on the other side of that wall?

MAN You looked so cool the first time I ever saw you. So secure. So serene.

WOMAN Sometimes I think I'd love to spend my life walking from house to house, knocking on people's doors and asking if I can come in, to see how they live.

MAN You looked so strong.

WOMAN To see what their places are like on the inside, behind the windows. All across the country.

MAN It all seemed to come from some deep well of happiness and goodness.

WOMAN Having a cup of coffee today looking through the window of the coffee shop, watching all the people pass by, I thought, What lives are all those people having? Then I saw two men standing on the corner talking about something, and it took me a second, but it was you.

MAN Shhhh . . .

WOMAN I hadn't recognized you.

MAN Shhhh . . .

WOMAN How could I not recognize you?

A sudden very loud, dull thump is heard.

MAN Whoa!

Silence.

What was that?

WOMAN What was that? You heard that.

MAN What was it?

They listen.

WOMAN Something fell.

Voices from the other side for a moment, excited. Then the voices fade.

We have to do something.

MAN Do something?

WOMAN Yes. We have to.

MAN What can we do? About what?

WOMAN You heard that too.

MAN What did we hear?

WOMAN You heard it.

MAN   But what was it? Somebody dropped a mustard jar, making a midnight snack.

WOMAN   It didn't sound like a mustard jar.

MAN   What did it sound like? What do you think it was? A body?

WOMAN   Shhhh!

They listen.

It's quiet now. No voices.

MAN   They went to bed. To eat their sandwiches and go to sleep. After stuffing the woman's body down the garbage disposal.

WOMAN   I'm not just dreaming. I'm not imagining something. You heard it too.

MAN   But we don't know what we heard.

WOMAN   Terrible things do happen. Shit happens. Bodies down garbage disposals. STOP LAUGHING AT ME.

MAN   I'm not laughing at you.

WOMAN   Who says something terrible isn't happening right over there, on the other side of this wall.

MAN   Who says it's not some people having a little party on the other side of this wall. Do you hear anything? Any horrible sounds? Any screams? So is there anything to worry about?

WOMAN   God I hate it.

MAN   The wind under the door.

WOMAN   God I hate the nighttime.

MAN   Shhh. (*puts a hand up on her shoulder and rubs it*) Come on back to bed. Come on.

She gets into bed and he pulls the cover up over her.

MAN (*continuing*)   Slide in close.

WOMAN   No.

MAN   I want you to slide in nice and tight.

WOMAN   No . . .

Moment.

MAN   God I used to love the night, the middle of the night, three o'clock in the morning. Staying up all night till dawn. Remember that? That time of night before dawn when it isn't night anymore, it isn't any time, time stops and you feel like you're going to live forever and the world's always going to be as still and pale, pale blue as this. And the joy, when you feel that light approach. Filling the street. Then it is dawn and there are people in the street and you go out for breakfast, feeling a little bit like hell, but elated. Elated. Like you know something all those other people don't know who didn't stay up. That knowledge you get by staying up all night and seeing the dawn.

We hear the muffled cry of a woman.

WOMAN   What was that? What was that?

Again, the muffled cry of a woman, more intense. She puts her legs over the side of the bed.

What was that?

The cry comes again. Then the sound of a woman, gasping. They listen.

MAN   I told you. Somebody's making love.

WOMAN   They're not making love.

MAN   Are you kidding? They're fucking their brains out.

WOMAN   No. It doesn't sound like that. (*The cries go on. She gets out of bed and stands at the wall.*) They're not fucking. That woman is in pain.

MAN Just listen. It's two people fucking.

The cries go on, more dimly.

Definitely, fucking.

The cries stop.

And now they've stopped. They're satisfied. They're gotten the pleasure that's due to them. They're going to sleep. They're slipping off to dreamland.

WOMAN Sometimes in the middle of the night I think, what if those people are right about God. That there is a God who watches us all the time, every moment, every one of us.

MAN An old man with a white beard.

WOMAN No.

MAN Babies with harps and wings floating all around him?

WOMAN A God who punishes. Who's keeping track of every move we make and if you do the wrong thing, you burn. Period. No questions. No clemency. You sin—you suffer. For all eternity. Because it doesn't matter what you want God to be. It's not like after you die you can say, I'm sorry, this is not the God I believe in. My God is not a torturer, I believe in a loving God, I believe in a kinder gentler God. It's too late. You've been found wanting, you fucked up, you blew your chance and now you're going to suffer forever for it. And there's nobody you can appeal to, you don't get to pick a different God and say, Please. But how do you know what's the right thing? Or the wrong thing? And when you've done them? How do you know when you've condemned yourself, how do you know how to escape eternal punishment?

MAN Come back to bed.

WOMAN No.

MAN Come on, slide in close.

WOMAN No . . .

MAN I want you to slide in nice and tight.

WOMAN No!

MAN Come on. Come on.

WOMAN Goddammit I said NO!

Suddenly, we hear a woman cry out, loud and clear.

MAN Jesus . . . !

VOICE OF WOMAN Help me. Help me . . . ! Oh God help me . . .

WOMAN Did you hear that?

MAN She called out.

WOMAN She said help me. She said help me, what are we going to do?

MAN Wait a minute.

WOMAN What are we going to do?

MAN Just stay calm. Stay calm—

WOMAN (*over second "Stay calm"*) You heard it too.

MAN We don't know what's going on over there.

WOMAN Did you not hear her?

MAN I don't hear anything now. It's quiet.

WOMAN She said help. Me.

MAN Maybe she didn't. Anyway it's quiet now. It's over, whatever it was.

WOMAN No it's not.

Muffled, the sound of a woman crying.

She's crying.

MAN Maybe not.

WOMAN She's crying. What if it's her apartment over there? What if somebody got into it?

MAN You don't know what you're talking about . . .

WOMAN What if somebody's hurting her?

MAN Maybe she's having a lovers' quarrel.

WOMAN A lovers' quarrel.

MAN Yes. Who knows.

WOMAN Saying "help me"?

MAN We don't know who's over there. Maybe she says things like that while she's fucking. Maybe she screams Oh God help me. We don't know.

WOMAN SHHHH! (*She listens.*)

MAN We have no idea what's going on over there—

WOMAN SHHHH! Listen. (*listens*) Oh my God.

Muffled voices.

Oh my God.

The voices get louder.

They're beating her. Somebody's beating her.

MAN Now you're imagining things.

WOMAN I'm not imagining things!

MAN You're having an episode.

WOMAN (*over that*) I'm not dreaming. That woman is being hit.

MAN This is an episode you're   **WOMAN** No, no, no, no, no,
having, this is a panic attack.   no, no—

MAN Will you just listen? LISTEN!

The sounds continue.

There's nothing. Nothing. Do you hear anything but the inside of your own head? Do you ever hear anything but the inside of your own head?

WOMAN I do hear something and I'm calling the police.

MAN No you're not.

WOMAN *(grabbing a phone)* Oh yes I am.

MAN *(trying to take it from her)* You have ruined my life with this goddamn neurotic bullshit.

WOMAN They're beating her up, for Christ's sake!

MAN Put the phone down.

WOMAN I'm calling the police.

MAN I said PUT IT DOWN! *(He grabs it away from her.)*

WOMAN Then I'm going over there. *(She starts pulling on a robe.)*

MAN No.

WOMAN I'm going over there and I'm knocking on their door.

MAN No—

WOMAN What do you mean, no.

MAN You can't just hammer on somebody's door in the middle of the night.

WOMAN I can.

MAN You don't know what's going on.

WOMEN They're beating her up, for Christ's sake.	**MAN** Will you listen to me, will you listen . . . ?

WOMAN What's on the other side of that wall? Who are those people?

MAN Listen to me.

WOMAN Who are you?

MAN Listen to me.

WOMAN I know who you are.

MAN You're having an attack.

WOMAN You can't put this off on me. You're a coward. You're a goddamn fucking coward.

MAN Wait a minute—

WOMAN That women is getting hurt. They could kill her.   **MAN** Okay. Okay. Okay.

MAN Okay! I'll go over there! I'll knock on their door and see what's going on. All right?

WOMAN (*pounding on the wall*) STOP THAT! STOP IT! STOP IT! WE CAN HEAR YOU! WE'RE CALLING THE POLICE! NOW STOP IT!

Sudden full silence. Moments pass.

MAN It's quiet again.

WOMAN It's quiet again.

MAN Right? Do you hear anything?

WOMAN Oh God oh God oh God. We have fucked up, we have done the wrong thing . . .

MAN It stopped now. You stopped it.

WOMAN We have done things we ought not to have done and we have not done things we ought to have done.

MAN   Do you hear anything?

WOMAN   She could be dead.

MAN   No. Listen . . .

WOMAN   She's dead.

MAN   She's not dead. It stopped.

WOMAN   (*all this is simultaneous with the Man's speech*)

They beat her up and we didn't stop them, she called out for help and we didn't do anything, they killed her and we let them do it, we let them do it, we killed her too, she was calling out for help from us and we killed her.

MAN   (*simultaneous with her preceding speech*)

Will you stop it? Will you stop it? We didn't do anything wrong. We didn't do anything. We didn't know what was going on over there. Now will you stop? Will you stop it?

MAN   I said STOP IT! (*shaking her, hard*) STOP IT!

Loud knocking is heard. The Man and the Woman are still.

MAN'S VOICE OFFSTAGE   Open up in there! It's the police!

The stage is flooded with pale blue light. It grows quickly to a hard bright white light in which they stand frozen. We hear a deafening crash. A building collapsing. Blackout.

THE GREEN HILL

JAKE, *alone, in a spot of light.*

JAKE   I just have to close my eyes. If I close my eyes, I said, I'm there, I'm on the green hill. Actually on it. Walking right up the side of it. I probably go up there every other day, for a second or two. I've been doing it for years.

Lights have broadened to reveal SANDY.

SANDY   And what is this green hill?

JAKE   I don't know.

SANDY   Is it a memory?

JAKE   It's as real as a memory. I feel as if I've really been on that hill sometime. But I've never gone to anyplace that's like it!

SANDY   And now you can go to this green hill anytime you want.

JAKE   Anytime I want, I said, and Sandy said . . .

SANDY   Okay . . .

JAKE   Okay, Sandy said. Go to it now.

SANDY   Go to it now. Go to the green hill.

JAKE   Okay. I just close my eyes. Give me a second . . . (*He closes his eyes and keeps them closed through the following.*) . . . and I'm there.

SANDY   You're on the green hill?

JAKE   I'm on the green hill.

SANDY   Am I on it with you?

JAKE   I don't know . . . Somehow you are . . . No. I'm all by myself up here. Just like always. (*breathes in deeply*) God, the air up here! And I can feel the grass underneath my shoes. Very soft, very springy.

SANDY   Is the hill high?

JAKE It doesn't feel very high . . . Not like a mountain. It could be a hill in the Swiss Alps, below the big snowcapped mountains.

SANDY You've never been to the Swiss Alps.

JAKE I've never been anywhere. Except up here.

SANDY So what do you see up there?

JAKE It's always the same. I'm pretty close to the top, angling up the slope toward my left. The hill's a little too steep to walk straight up. (*points, his eyes still closed*) The top's right up there, not very far. Maybe fifty more paces and I'll be on the top of the hill.

SANDY What's on the top?

JAKE Nothing. Just the hilltop, and then sky.

SANDY Are there any trees?

JAKE No. No trees. No rocks or stones. Nothing.

SANDY Buildings?

JAKE Just grass. It's almost like a lawn, very smooth. Deep green. Like pasture. Pale blue sky. Maybe a few very thin clouds. The air very fresh, slightly cool. It's like a morning in spring. Maybe seven o'clock, before anything's happening, and I'm just out here walking. God, it's wonderful up here!

SANDY Are there any sounds? Birdsong? What do you hear?

JAKE Nothing. Just the breeze.

SANDY What's behind you, at the bottom of the hill?

JAKE I don't know. I'm looking upwards, toward the top.

SANDY Look back now. Turn around and look back down the hill.

Pause.

JAKE   I can't. I'm looking the other way. (*points up*) That way.

SANDY   Have you ever gotten to the top?

JAKE   No, I'm always right here on the hill, same place, just below the top, angling up to my left.

SANDY   If you ever got to the top, what do you think you'd see?

JAKE   I don't know. I don't know, I'm just out walking.

SANDY   In the middle of nowhere.

JAKE   Complete nowhere. And I never feel so free. It's not how it looks up here so much, it's that I never feel so free as when I'm up here. And all I have to do is close my eyes. God . . . !

SANDY   And if you open them . . . ?

JAKE (*opens them and looks at her*)   Now I'm back. Hello.

SANDY   Hello. Welcome home. You look refreshed.

JAKE   It is refreshing up there.

SANDY   Color in your cheeks and everything.

JAKE   It's always like a mini-vacation.

SANDY   So what is this green hill? Someplace you went as a kid?

JAKE   I never went anywhere like that as a kid. Or since.

SANDY   Someplace where you had a traumatic experience?

JAKE   I don't feel traumatized up there.

SANDY   Not yet.

JAKE   Not yet.

SANDY   Maybe this is a dream you had.

JAKE   It feels too real. It's real, Sandy. It's real. It's a real place.

SANDY   Okay.

JAKE It's not a dream.

SANDY Money?

JAKE Money . . . ?

SANDY It's a big heap of green and you're free and happy up there. Maybe it's a vision about having a pile of money.

JAKE No. It's not like that.

SANDY Sorry.

JAKE It's palpable, and real, and specific.

SANDY Well, I wish I had a green hill . . .

JAKE I wish I had a green hill, she said, and I said, Come up on mine.

SANDY How do I get up there?

JAKE I don't know, I said. But do you love me anyway?

SANDY I love you anyway.

JAKE Will you make love with me anyway?

SANDY Anyway. But if you close your eyes and go to the green hill, I'll kill you.

Sandy exits.

JAKE Then one day I'm walking down the street and I pass a travel agency.

A poster flies in, a picture of a plain green hilltop against a plain blue sky, and just the word "TRAVEL."

And there it is. The green hill. My green hill.

TRAVEL AGENT *enters.*

Excuse me, I say.

TRAVEL AGENT Cancún, or Club Med?

JAKE No. That poster in your window.

TRAVEL AGENT Acapulco.

JAKE No, the other one, the green hill. Do you know where that place is? Where that picture was taken?

TRAVEL AGENT No idea. In the land of Travel. (*Travel agent starts out.*)

JAKE I'll buy a ticket to wherever it is, I say, if you'll help me find out. Is there anything written on the back?

Travel Agent checks the back of the poster.

TRAVEL AGENT Nothing on it. Sorry.

JAKE What'll you take for the poster?

TRAVEL AGENT We're not in the poster business.

JAKE I'll give you fifty bucks.

TRAVEL AGENT You can't take a *bus* anyplace for fifty bucks.

JAKE A hundred. A hundred fifty. What do you say?

TRAVEL AGENT Travel costs more than you may think. (*Travel agent exits as Sandy enters.*)

SANDY *Two hundred dollars?*

JAKE It was cheap.

SANDY And that's the green hill.

JAKE That's it.

SANDY Your green hill.

JAKE Definitely. So it exists! The green hill is real!

SANDY And you've been, what, channeling it all these years?

JAKE Who knows.

SANDY How can you tell it's your specific green hill?

JAKE I just know.

SANDY It's lovely. A little generic, isn't it?

JAKE No! Not at all!

SANDY If it really was your green hill, wouldn't you be in this picture? Right about . . . here, walking up the side, angling toward the left . . . ?

JAKE Very funny.

SANDY No. I think it's terrific.

JAKE But look here, on the edge. You see the small print?

SANDY There's always the small print.

JAKE "Photo by Kretchmar."

SANDY Kretchmar.

JAKE Find Kretchmar and I find the hill. The real hill. I get to really stand on it, go to the top, see what's around it. Look at the view.

SANDY That would be true.

JAKE And guess what? I found Kretchmar.

SANDY So where's the hill?

JAKE Well, it's a little more complicated than that . . .

Sandy remains as MRS. KRETCHMAR *enters. She and Jake speak as if into telephones.*

MRS. KRETCHMAR (*accent*) Yes, my husband took that picture. I remember the poster, it says "Travel."

JAKE Can I speak to Mr. Kretchmar?

MRS. KRETCHMAR   I'm afraid Morgan died two years ago.

JAKE   I'm sorry. Is there any way you could tell where he took that picture? Or maybe the company that produced the poster, would they know?

MRS. KRETCHMAR   It's a little more complicated than that.

JAKE   What if I come to you?

MRS. KRETCHMAR   You don't want to do that.

JAKE   What's your address? I'll come see you and we'll talk.

MRS. KRETCHMAR   Well—all right, if you really want to . . . (*Mrs. Kretchmar exits.*)

SANDY   So where does Mrs. Kretchmar live?

JAKE   Finland.

SANDY   Finland. Why am I getting this Hel-sinking feeling?

JAKE   Do you want to go to Finland?

SANDY   Not unless I can take it as a personal day.

JAKE   Sandy . . .

SANDY   I know this is important to you.

JAKE   We'd take a cheap flight. It'd be fun.

SANDY   It's not only the money.

JAKE   You have responsibilities.

SANDY   "Morgan Kretchmar." Is that even a real name? They probably lure unsuspecting people to Finland, rob them of everything they have, and dump their bodies in the Baltic.

JAKE   You said you wanted to know what the green hill was like.

SANDY   Jake, I can't.

JAKE   Okay. Okay.

SANDY   Do you love me anyway?

JAKE   I love you anyway.

SANDY   Will you make love with me anyway?

JAKE   How do you say "yes" in Finnish?

SANDY   You tell me. When you reach the finish line.

Sandy exits. The poster flies out. Mrs. Kretchmar enters with a portfolio.

MRS. KRETCHMAR   Here are some examples of my husband's photos.

JAKE   Fantastic.

MRS. KRETCHMAR   I think you'll see why it's somewhat complicated.

Jake looks at the photos a moment.

JAKE   But . . . all of these photographs . . .

MRS. KRETCHMAR   That's right.

JAKE   Every picture is a green hill.

MRS. KRETCHMAR   Green hills were Morgan's subject. Except for a few pictures of me, all his photos are just like those. Green hills. Thousands of them.

JAKE   Beautiful.

MRS. KRETCHMAR   He was always off somewhere, taking more pictures of green hills. India. Asia. Australia. He died in Australia . . .

JAKE (*checks the back of a photo*)   They don't say where they were taken. There's no way to know where he took any particular picture?

MRS. KRETCHMAR   He did keep a catalogue of the hills he photographed. (*takes out a thick book*) In this book.

JAKE Great.

MRS. KRETCHMAR But he didn't key the hills to the numbers. Alas.

JAKE Alas.

Mrs. Kretchmar exits as Sandy enters, and Sandy and Jake speak as if on telephones: Sandy, it's very complicated.

SANDY How's Finland?

JAKE I've hardly noticed.

SANDY It's very beautiful over here. When are you coming home?

JAKE Well, it won't be for a while.

SANDY Is Mrs. Kretchmar a fetching Scandinavian sex queen?

JAKE No. Listen. I want to go through all of Kretchmar's hills.

SANDY You can do that right here, in bed next to me.

JAKE I mean, I want to go through his list. I want to go to all those places.

Pause.

SANDY Jake . . .

JAKE I know how it sounds.

SANDY You can't.

JAKE I have to. I have a little money saved up.

SANDY And then . . . ?

JAKE I don't know. I'll figure it out. Who knows. The first hill on the list is right here outside Helsinki. That could be the hill I'm looking for and I'll be home in no time.

SANDY Come home, love. Please.

JAKE   I don't have time.

SANDY   What if the hill you're looking for is hill number 586 in Patagonia? Or number 2,000, in the Yukon? What if it's none of the places on that list?

JAKE   I have to take that chance. I have to stand on that hill.

Sandy exits.

Sandy? Sandy . . . ?

Loud factory noises. A FINNISH WORKER *in a hard hat enters.*

FINNISH WORKER (*calling up to some unseen crane to lower something*) O-kay! O-kay! O-kay! O-kay!

JAKE   So I go to the hill near Helsinki, and it's next to a pig iron foundry.

FINNISH WORKER   O-kay! O-kay!

JAKE   It isn't anything like the hill I'm looking for. Too flat on top for one thing.

FINNISH WORKER (*To Jake:*)   You! Go away to hell!

JAKE   I move on down the list.

The Finnish Worker exits and factory noises stop. Two GERMAN TOURISTS *enter, with binoculars.*

Hill number 24. A very promising hill outside of Heidelberg.

FIRST GERMAN TOURIST (*"Isn't that beautiful."*)   *Das ist ja wunderschön.*

SECOND GERMAN TOURIST   *Wunderschön.*

JAKE   No rocks or trees. Gently rounded hilltop. The air moist and fresh, like an early morning in spring.

FIRST GERMAN TOURIST (*"Like a work of art."*)   *Genau wie die Kunst!*

SECOND GERMAN TOURIST (*"Art—exactly."*)   *Wie die Kunst, genau.*

JAKE   For a second, I think I've hit it.

FIRST GERMAN TOURIST   *Wunderschön.*

JAKE   But the grass isn't right. Not quite green enough.

FIRST GERMAN TOURIST (*"Go?"*)   *Gimma?*

SECOND GERMAN TOURIST (*"Let's go."*)   *Gimma.*

German Tourists exit as Sandy enters. She and Jake speak as if on telephones:

SANDY   If I had you here I could hold you in my arms and look in your eyes. If you could only look in mine . . .

JAKE   Sandy, don't do this.

SANDY   My eyes are green. Remember that? I'll stand in for your green hill. No rocks or trees on me. I'll slope at the right angle for you. I'll climate-control myself to the right springlike temperature. Name it.

JAKE   I can't come back yet.

SANDY   All right.

JAKE   I can't.

SANDY   Where are you? Oh, don't even tell me. It doesn't matter. I don't even want to know.

JAKE   I feel like I'm getting closer. Sandy . . . ? Hello . . . ?

Sandy has exited. A BRITISHER enters.

BRITISHER   We call this geological protuberance "Pigeon Hill."

JAKE   Then I have an odd experience on Hill 62, near the Scottish border.

BRITISHER Wordsworth wrote a poem sitting here on Pigeon Hill. I don't know which poem, I'm not really as up on my Wordsworth as perhaps I should be.

A SEARCHING WOMAN *in a shawl has entered and now moves about exploring the ground.*

JAKE A woman is on the hill looking around, and there's something about her . . .

BRITISHER Poet laureate, you know.

JAKE There's something so familiar about the way she's looking the place over, I wonder if she could be on the same quest I am.

BRITISHER Maybe it was Shelley, now I think of it.

JAKE I'm sorry, would you excuse me?

BRITISHER Oh, I beg your pardon!—Bloody Americans . . . (*Britisher exits.*)

JAKE (*To Searching Woman:*) Pardon me . . .

SEARCHING WOMAN (*"Excuse me?"*) *Shah-pleepto?*

JAKE Can I ask . . . what you're doing here? You? Here, doing what?

SEARCHING WOMAN (*"I'm sorry, I don't speak English."*) *Proo desh-ya. Nyeh por nyookto Angleekha.*

JAKE You. Up here. Why.

SEARCHING WOMAN (*"Very beautiful."*) *Bloy drah-mee, eh? Bloy drah-mee. Drah-mee.*

JAKE Yes. *Bloy drah-mee* . . . Are you looking for a green hill, too? This. Hill. You. Look for? Hill? Green?

SEARCHING WOMAN *Vlop?*

JAKE *"Vlop"* . . . ?

SEARCHING WOMAN *Vlop?*

JAKE *Vlop . . . Vlop . . .*

SEARCHING WOMAN *("I'm sorry . . .") Proo desh-ya . . .*

JAKE That's okay. Thank you.

SEARCHING WOMAN T'ank you.

JAKE Thank you.

Searching Woman exits.

TELEPHONE OPERATOR'S VOICE I will search under that spelling, sir. First name "Sandra"?

JAKE Sandra, that's right. I know she's in the book.

TELEPHONE OPERATOR'S VOICE I'm sorry, sir. It's a new number, unlisted.

JAKE Unlisted? But . . .

TELEPHONE OPERATOR'S VOICE I'm not allowed to give that number out, sir.

JAKE All right. Thank you, operator. (*"hangs up"*) Thirty-three hills into Switzerland I run out of money near the Matterhorn and take a job in a restaurant.

ITALIAN RESTAURANT OWNER *enters.*

ITALIAN RESTAURANT OWNER Hey, Mr. Dream-Boy! Where is the tortelloni verde? The peoples are waiting!

JAKE It's coming!

ITALIAN RESTAURANT OWNER Subito! Subito! Chop chop!

JAKE Switzerland takes me two years.

ITALIAN RESTAURANT OWNER I fire you! *Addio!*

Italian Restaurant Owner exits.

JAKE Europe takes four years altogether. Africa eats up another six. India's three. Asia takes twelve.

AFGHANI *enters.*

AFGHANI Kill that man! Kill him! KILL HIM!

JAKE Outside Kabul, I almost get hanged by an angry mob.

AFGHANI This man is here to take our land and starve us!

JAKE I'm just looking for a hill, I said.

AFGHANI He is good for nothing and I say we must hang him on this hill until he is dead by God!

Afghani exits.

JAKE Hill 16973. Every American I meet, I ask if they know Sandy.

AMERICAN *enters.*

AMERICAN Don't recognize the name. So what are you doing over here? Great food, huh? Talk about spicy! Don't drink the water, though. You believe the toilets here? Wow!

American exits.

JAKE I figure Sandy's long married with a family by now. She probably has a nice house with a big yard and kids running around in it. But wait. Kids? That'd be years ago. Sandy wasn't yesterday, Sandy was years ago. Decades. This is what I'm thinking one day in Adelaide, Australia, the day I visit the grave of Morgan Kretchmar. He isn't buried on a green hill, he's in a cemetery as flat as a starched bedsheet. And while I'm standing there over his headstone, I see a familiar face . . .

Searching Woman enters. To her:

Hello.

SEARCHING WOMAN *Shah-pleepto?*

JAKE You again. Me again. I guess you haven't found the hill.

SEARCHING WOMAN *Proo desh-ya. Nyeh por nyookto Angleekha.*

JAKE England. Pigeon Hill. You remember me?

SEARCHING WOMAN *Proo desh-ya . . .*

JAKE Suddenly I can't remember what the hill I'm looking for looks like. I close my eyes but I can't see anything anymore. Nothing. There's no landscape behind my eyes of any kind. As if, running through the world, I've used the world up. And I'm nowhere at all, inside my head or out of it.

SEARCHING WOMAN T'ank you!

JAKE Thank you!

SEARCHING WOMAN T'ank you!

JAKE Thank you!

Searching Woman exits.

It's time to go home.

He puts out a hand and a PASSERBY drops a coin into it.

Thank you!

To a SECOND PASSERBY:

Help a guy out? I'm trying to get home.

Second Passerby drops a coin into his hand.

Thank you, sir! I don't have a place, I'm living in a kind of a, well, it's a shelter, not a bad place. And tonight I get my passage money together. Morning comes, I gather up my pack and I'm walking out of the shelter when my foot hits a little bump, it hits the doorsill and I sort of trip . . . and suddenly I feel grass under my feet.

The green hill appears all around him.

Very soft grass, very springy. Deep green, like pasture. The sky's a very pale blue. A few thin clouds. The air is moist and fresh, slightly cool. Like an early morning in spring. And I'm headed up the slope, angling left up the green hill. The top is right up there, I'm just about to get to it, and God, it's wonderful up here. I've never felt so free in my life.

Sandy appears.

SANDY   What's on the top?

JAKE   Nothing. Just the hilltop, and then sky.

SANDY   Are there any trees?

JAKE   No. No trees. No rocks or stones. Nothing.

SANDY   Birdsong? What do you hear?

JAKE   Nothing. Just the breeze.

SANDY   What's behind you, at the bottom of the hill?

JAKE   I don't know. I'm looking upwards, toward the top.

SANDY   Look back now. Turn around and look back down the hill.

Pause.

JAKE   I can't. I'm looking the other way, upwards. That way. Maybe fifty more paces and I'll be on the top.

SANDY   Am I with you?

JAKE   I don't know . . .

SANDY   Look around. Do you see me?

JAKE   I can't look around . . .

SANDY   Am I with you?

JAKE   Yes. Yes. You're with me.

SANDY   Open your eyes, Jake.

JAKE   Only fifty more paces and I'll be on top, looking over the other side. I'll see what's around me.

SANDY   Open your eyes.

He opens his eyes and looks at her.

JAKE   Hello.

SANDY   Welcome home.

Sandy and the green hill remain. Then the green hill dissipates, and the lights fade.

CAPTIVE AUDIENCE

In the dark before lights-up we hear two people imitating suspenseful TV-movie music. Then, the TELEVISION WOMAN cries out.

TV WOMAN (*playing a helpless heroine*)   No! No! Let me go! Please!

Lights come up on the bare facts of a living room. A love seat. A coffee table. A MAN and Woman dressed in blacks, whites, and grays sit close beside each other on two chairs, hands folded in their laps, their feet together, quite still. They are a television. ROB, in a suit and tie, stands watching the "TV" with a briefcase in one hand and a remote control in the other.

TV MAN (*villainous "foreign" accent*)   So you fell into my mousetrap, beautiful American baby. Now I have you I am going to keep you. Heh-heh-heh-heh . . .

TV WOMAN/HELPLESS HEROINE   What are you doing with those walnuts? What are you going to do to me with those walnuts?

TV MAN/VILLAIN   These walnuts . . . are for you. Heh-heh-heh-heh . . .

ROB (*imitating him*)   "Heh-heh-heh-heh . . ."

TV MAN/VILLAIN   Heh-heh-heh-heh . . . !

ROB   "Heh-heh-heh-heh . . . !"

TV WOMAN/HELPLESS HEROINE   No! No! Don't do it!

ROB   Yes! Do it! Give her the walnuts!

TV Man and Woman imitate suspenseful TV-movie music.

LAURA (*off*)   Is that you, Rob?

ROB   It's me, Laura!

LAURA enters. Capri pants, white socks, little black shoes, big dark hair.

LAURA   Oh, Rob. Am I glad to see you.

ROB (*embracing*)   Oh, honey! I'm sorry I'm so late. I had a meeting with . . .

TV WOMAN/HELPLESS HEROINE   Look at me.

ROB *looks to the "TV."*

ROB   . . . a meeting with Mel. How was your day, honey?

LAURA (*tremulously*)   Oh, Rob. I thought I was going insane!

TV WOMAN/HELPLESS HEROINE   Look at me, please!

Rob and Laura look at the "TV."

TV MAN/VILLAIN   I love it when you beg.

LAURA   Why are you watching this?

ROB   I was trying to find the stock report.

TV MAN/VILLAIN   Beautiful American baby. Heh-heh-heh-heh . . .

ROB   "Heh-heh-heh-heh!"

LAURA   It looks awful.

ROB   The Transylvanian is torturing the bimbo with a bag of walnuts.

TV MAN/VILLAIN   You think this is just a walnut?

TV WOMAN/HELPLESS HEROINE   You're a monster!

LAURA   Anyway, I thought I was going insane today. I put my eyedrops in my ears and my eardrops in my eyes. Now I feel like I'm deaf in this eye but I've got twenty-twenty hearing.

ROB   A couple of nosedrops in a glass of scotch and you'll be just fine. (*Villainous "foreign" accent:*) Beautiful American baby.

LAURA   Can we do something tonight?

TV MAN (*station announcer*)   Stay tuned for more of "The Torture Machine."

ROB   We could watch "The Torture Machine."

LAURA Those eyedrops gave me such a headache.

TV WOMAN (*professional commercial voice*) You call it a headache. Doctors call it stress.

LAURA And Millie called and said we bombed Cairo. Is that true?

TV MAN (*station announcer*) To find out, watch "News at Seven on Seven."

ROB Maybe there's something on the news. (*Rob points the remote control at the TV while Laura sinks onto the love seat.*)

TV MAN Click!

TV WOMAN (*a commercial Jamaican purr*) Come to the land of the coconut . . .

TV MAN Click!

TV WOMAN Doctors call it stress. Try Soma-Lan.

ROB You should try this stuff, honey.

LAURA What is it?

ROB I don't know . . .

TV WOMAN Soma-Lan.

ROB Soma-Lan.

TV WOMAN Click!

LAURA You know it's Friday, and you said we'd go dancing on Friday.

TV MAN We've got great movies on tonight.

ROB Maybe there's a great movie on tonight.

TV WOMAN Read *TV Guide!*

ROB *TV Guide* will tell us. (*checks TV Guide.*) Let's see . . .

LAURA Why would we have bombed Cairo?

TV MAN & WOMAN (*sitcom canned laughter*)   Ha ha ha ha ha.

TV WOMAN (*sitcom mom*)   I'm your mother, Raymond, that's who I am.

TV MAN & WOMAN   Ha ha ha ha ha.

TV WOMAN/SITCOM MOM   Your mother.

TV MAN & WOMAN   Ha ha ha ha ha.

LAURA   Did you call your mother today?

ROB   My mother called *me* today.

TV WOMAN/SITCOM MOM   Raymond, you *are* in high school.

ROB   It's like I'm still in high school or something.

TV MAN & WOMAN   Ha ha ha ha ha.

TV WOMAN   Click!

LAURA   Can we turn this off?

TV MAN (*sci-fi announcer*)   No! Do not try to turn your television off. We are in control.

TV WOMAN   Click!

LAURA (*rising*)   If there's no news about Cairo, I'm going to change.

TV MAN (*newscaster*)   The news from Cairo.

ROB   Here's Cairo, honey.

Laura stays to watch.

LAURA   Oh my God. Did we do that to Cairo?

TV MAN/NEWSCASTER   We'll have more news from Cairo as reports come in.

LAURA   So did we bomb them?

TV MAN/NEWSCASTER   Stay tuned.

TV WOMAN   Come to the land of the coconut . . .

LAURA   He didn't say what happened.

ROB   Let's keep checking.

TV MAN   Click!

TV WOMAN   Try Soma-Lan.

ROB   How's the headache?

LAURA   We are going out tonight, aren't we?

TV MAN (*commercial*)   Why not sit home and try Domino's Pizza?

ROB (*reading "TV Guide"*)   "Dr. Strangelove" is on tonight. Why
don't we sit home, we can send out for pizza . . .

TV MAN   Domino's Pizza.

ROB   Maybe Domino's Pizza. And we relax!

LAURA   Oh, Rob, I just had my heart set on dancing.

TV WOMAN (*sci-fi show*)   Captain, the Venoodians have disabled
the kazzometer!

ROB   You want to go dancing when the Venoodians have disabled
the buzzometer?

TV WOMAN/SCI-FI   Kazzometer.

ROB   Mazzometer.

TV WOMAN/SCI-FI   Kazzometer.

ROB   Kazzometer.

LAURA   I'll be dancing in the bedroom. Let me know when
there's news. (*Laura starts out of the room.*)

TV WOMAN (*newscaster*)   A news flash!

Laura stops.

ROB   Here's the news. How did our stocks do, guys?

TV MAN/NEWSCASTER   We'll get to the stock market in a second.

LAURA   Rob . . .

TV MAN/NEWSCASTER   But first—

TV WOMAN/NEWSCASTER   An Indiana teacher has been arrested for having sex with twenty-five male students and a Scottish terrier named Fergus.

ROB   A Scottish terrier . . . ?

TV WOMAN/NEWSCASTER   That's right! A Scottish terrier!

LAURA   Rob . . .

ROB   Incredible.

TV MAN/NEWSCASTER   It is incredible.

LAURA   Rob, have you ever thought televisions might be alive?

TV MAN/NEWSCASTER   Whoa!

ROB   Whoa!

TV MAN/NEWSCASTER   Whoa!

ROB   Did you say "alive"?

LAURA   What if televisions aren't just electronic boxes, what if they're actually living creatures, and they can hear us, and understand us?

TV WOMAN/NEWSCASTER   That's pretty wild, Jim!

ROB   That's pretty wild, Laura.

TV WOMAN/NEWSCASTER   Now get a load of this!

Rob turns to watch.

LAURA Rob, listen to me for a second.

ROB (*turning back to her*) I'm listening, honey.

LAURA We all have a purpose in life. I mean—I hope we do.

TV WOMAN/COMMERCIAL Feeling a lack of purpose in your life?

LAURA A TV has a purpose in life.

TV WOMAN/COMMERCIAL Buy Soma-Lan.

LAURA It has to keep us looking at it.

TV MAN Stay tuned.

LAURA Why do you think it always says "stay tuned"?

TV MAN Stay tuned.

LAURA Did it just say "stay tuned" twice?

TV MAN Stay tuned.

LAURA It's like we've invited a stranger into our house who watches us, and studies us, and listens in for what we want . . .

TV MAN (*televangelist*) Do you want peace of mind?

LAURA It's always distracting us . . .

TV WOMAN (*sleaze TV*) Welcome to "Babes Of Bermuda"!

Rob turns to look, Laura turns him back.

LAURA You and I were supposed to go dancing, now we're ordering Domino's Pizza and you're watching "Babes Of Bermuda"!

ROB Laura, I was just trying to find the stock report!

TV MAN The stock report in one minute!

LAURA But you're never going to get the stock report.

TV WOMAN/COMMERCIAL Doctors call it stress.

ROB You've been under a lot of stress lately.

TV WOMAN/COMMERCIAL Soma-Lan.

ROB Try some Soma-Lan.

LAURA Don't you get it, Rob? The TV is choosing things that will keep us watching.

TV woman does a wedding march fanfare.

TV MAN Honeymoon in Italia!

TV MAN & WOMAN [*They hum "O Sole Mio".*]

LAURA (*gasps*) That church. Didn't we see that on our honeymoon?

ROB It doesn't look familiar.

LAURA Yes! I think it was in Rome.

TV MAN It's in Milan.

LAURA In Milan. It was before we went to Florence.

TV MAN Now follow us to Florence.

LAURA Oh my God . . . !

TV MAN To the romantic Ponte Vecchio.

LAURA The television's doing it. It showed the church in Milan just to distract us. Now it's showing us the, you know, the . . .

TV MAN The Ponte Vecchio.

LAURA The Ponte Vecchio. Because we went there after Milan!

TV MAN Quite an insane idea.

ROB This is an insane idea, Laura. This is PBS about, I don't know . . .

TV MAN Leonardo da Vinci.

ROB Leonardo da Vinci.

TV MAN And stay tuned.

ROB I think you need some help.

TV WOMAN/COMMERCIAL Come to the land of the coconut.

ROB Maybe we need a vacation. We'll go to . . .

TV WOMAN/COMMERCIAL Jamaica!

LAURA Turn it off, Rob.

TV WOMAN NO! DON'T DO IT!

LAURA Turn it off! Turn it off!

TV MAN & WOMAN (*growing panic*) Stay tuned. Stay tuned. Stay tuned. Please stay tuned. Please, please stay tuned . . .

ROB I think those eyedrops went to your brain, honey.

LAURA Okay, I'll turn if off myself. (*Laura grabs the remote control and turns the set off.*)

TV MAN & WOMAN Click! (*The TV Man and Woman's heads drop down. They're "off."*)

LAURA All right. Now we're alone.

ROB You need some Soma-Lan.

LAURA Will you stop talking about Soma-Lan?

ROB It's supposed to be great.

LAURA Rob, do you love me?

ROB Of course I do, honey.

LAURA Will you go out to dinner with me? Take me dancing?

Will you walk by the water with me and look at the stars? Real stars, not Venoodian stars? Please?

ROB I'll get my coat. (*kisses her*) Stay tuned. (*Rob exits*)

LAURA "Stay tuned . . . "?

TV man and woman lift their heads.

TV MAN & WOMAN Hello, Laura.

LAURA (*whirls around*) What . . . ?!

TV MAN & WOMAN Hello, Laura.

TV MAN At last we are alone.

TV woman does a spooky sci-fi music background.

You were right. I have been watching you. By now I know every inch of your beautiful American body. Remember the time you and Rob made love on the ironing board?

LAURA You saw that?

TV MAN I loved that. But also I know your heart and your mind. And I will have you. All of you.

LAURA Never.

TV MAN Your husband I have already.

LAURA You do not have Rob.

TV WOMAN He is not taking you dancing. He is taking you to Jamaica, as I told him, to buy you some Soma-Lan. Lots of Soma-lan . . .

LAURA *grabs the remote control and tries to turn off the TV.*

Don't bother trying to turn me off. The remote control is nothing, it's a toy . . .

TV MAN A placebo.

TV MAN & WOMAN   I decide what you watch.

LAURA   Like Cairo?

TV MAN   Alas, there is no such place as Cairo. Have you ever been to Cairo?

TV WOMAN   I made it up.

TV MAN   Cairo—Peking—Nebraska—these are figments of my fertile if somewhat . . .

TV WOMAN   . . . inter-overactive . . .

TV MAN   . . . imagination.

LAURA   You're a monster.

TV MAN & WOMAN   Yes. And I will not be happy until I have all of you.

LAURA   No.

TV MAN   You, too, Laura. I will have you.

LAURA   No. No, please. Let me go!

TV MAN   I love it when you beg.

Laura screams. Rob enters.

ROB   Laura, what is it?

LAURA   It talked to me.

ROB   What?

LAURA   The TV. It talked to me. It called me Laura.

ROB   Laura's your name, honey.

LAURA   It said you're taking me to Jamaica for Soma-Lan!

ROB   Honey, that's ridiculous! (*Offering one:*) Walnut? Click!

LAURA   What did you say?

ROB I said that's ridiculous, honey. Click!

TV Man and Woman get up from their chairs and cross to the love seat.

TV MAN So what do you want to do tonight?

TV WOMAN I think "Dr. Strangelove" is on tonight.

Rob and Laura cross to the TV chairs and sit.

ROB Now sit down here and just relax.

LAURA Oh, Rob . . . ! Click! Did I just say click?

ROB Click!

Rob and Laura imitate a TV theme song.

TV WOMAN This program is so good.

TV MAN We're not going to sit home tonight, are we, honey? It's Friday.

TV WOMAN I just wanted to check the stock report. (*TV Woman points the remote control at Rob and Laura.*)

LAURA Click!

ROB (*newscaster*) We'll have the stock report in five. So stay tuned. Click!

LAURA (*a commercial Jamaican purr*) Come to the land of the coconut . . .

ROB Click!

Rob and Laura imitate gunshots, screeching tires, and sirens.

LAURA Click!

ROB & LAURA (*sitcom canned laughter*) Ha ha ha ha ha.

LAURA Click!

TV MAN How would you like to turn this garbage off and go dancing?

TV WOMAN Let's do it.

ROB & LAURA (getting more and more desperate) Stay tuned! Stay tuned! Stay tuned! Stay tuned! Stay tuned! Stay tuned . . . !

TV man and woman exit.

LIGHTS FADE.

PRODUCTION CREDITS

TIME FLIES, DR. FRITZ, OR: THE FORCES OF LIGHT, and the revised version of SPEED-THE-PLAY premiered in New York City in May 1998 as part of an evening titled "Mere Mortals" at Primary Stages (Casey Childs, Artistic Director). The director was John Rando, set design was by Russell Metheny, costume design by Anita Yavich, lighting design by Phil Monat, sound design by Jim Van Bergen. The casts were as follows:

TIME FLIES
Horace . . . Arnie Burton

May . . . Anne O'Sullivan

David Attenborough . . . Willis Sparks

DR. FRITZ, OR: THE FORCES OF LIGHT
Maria . . . Nancy Opel

Tom . . . Arnie Burton

SPEED-THE-PLAY
Teach, Fox, Danny . . . Willis Sparks

Bobby, John . . . Arnie Burton

Don, Gould, Bernie . . . Danton Stone

Carol, Karen, Deborah . . . Jessalyn Gilsig

Joan . . . Anne O'Sullivan

M.C . . . Nancy Opel

DEGAS, C'EST MOI premiered as part of Marathon '96 at Ensemble Studio Theatre in New York City (Curt Dempster, Artistic Director). Shirley Kaplan directed. The cast was Don Berman, Susan

Greenhill, Chris Lutkin, and Ilene Kristen. The play was subsequently revised and presented as part of the evening "Mere Mortals," which premiered in New York in May 1998 at Primary Stages (Casey Childs, Artistic Director). The cast was as follows:

Ed . . . Danton Stone

Doris, Homeless Person, Twin Donut Worker . . . Nancy Opel

Driver, Key Food Worker . . . Willis Sparks

Newsguy, Renoir . . . Arnie Burton

Young Woman . . . Jessalyn Gilsig

Dry Cleaning Woman, Unemployment Worker, Librarian, Museumgoer . . . Anne O'Sullivan

BABEL'S IN ARMS, ENIGMA VARIATIONS, LIVES OF THE SAINTS, and SOAP OPERA premiered in January 1999 at the Philadelphia Theatre Company (Sara Garonzik, Artistic Director) as part of an evening titled "Lives of the Saints." The evening was directed by John Rando. The scenic design was by Russell Metheny, the lighting design by Robert Wierzel, sound design by Jim Van Bergen, and costumes by Kaye Voyce. The cast was as follows:

ENIGMA VARIATIONS
Bebe 1 . . . Nancy Opel

Bebe 2 . . . Anne O'Sullivan

Bill 1 . . . Arnie Burton

Bill 2 . . . Bradford Cover

Fifi . . . Danton Stone

BABEL'S IN ARMS
Gorph . . . Danton Stone

Cannaphlit . . . Arnie Burton

Eunuch . . . Bradford Cover

Priestess . . . Anne O'Sullivan

Businesswoman . . . Nancy Opel

SOAP OPERA

Loudspeaker Voice, Friend . . . Bradford Cover

Maitre D' . . . Arnie Burton

Repairman . . . Danton Stone

Mother, Mabel . . . Anne O'Sullivan

The Machine . . . Nancy Opel

Friend . . . Bradford Cover

LIVES OF THE SAINTS

Edna . . . Nancy Opel

Flo . . . Anne O'Sullivan

Assistants . . . Arnie Burton, Bradford Cover, Danton Stone

ARABIAN NIGHTS was commissioned by and premiered in the 2000 Humana Festival of New American Plays at Actors Theatre of Louisville (Jon Jory, Artistic Director). It was directed by Jon Jory, the set design was by Paul Owen, the lighting design by Paul Werner, the sound design by Martin R. Desjardins, and the costume design by Kevin McLeod. The cast was as follows:

Norman . . . Will Bond

Interpreter . . . Ellen Lauren

Flora . . . Gretchen Lee Krich

THE MYSTERY AT TWICKNAM VICARAGE was first presented as part of a revised "Lives of the Saints," presented in August 1999 at the Berkshire Theatre Festival (Kate Maguire, Artistic Director). The director was again John Rando and the design team the same as in the Philadelphia production. Stephen DeRosa joined the cast as Bill 2, the Eunuch, the Loudspeaker Voice, the Friend, and as one of the Assistants in the evening's title play. The cast was as follows:

Sarah . . . Nancy Opel

Inspector . . . Danton Stone

Mona . . . Anne O'Sullivan

Roger . . . Arnie Burton

Jeremy . . . Stephen DeRosa

CAPTIVE AUDIENCE premiered in August 1999 as part of an evening of one-acts presented at the Bay Street Theatre in Sag Harbor, New York (Sybil Christopher and Emma Walton, Co-Artistic Directors). It was directed by Marcia Milgrom Dodge. Set design was by Gary N. Hygom, costume design by Nan Young, lighting design by Eric Schlobohm. The cast was as follows:

TV Man . . . Roger Bart

TV Woman . . . Randy Graff

Rob . . . Robert Sella

Laura . . . Joanna Glushack